The Prithviwallahs

for Jennifer

Acknowledgements

I, and all of us at Prithvi Theatre, would like to convey our deepest thanks to all those who have been part of this journey over the past twenty-five years—playwrights, producers, directors, actors, technicians, volunteers, media persons, and most importantly our avid and faithful audience. I would also like to thank all the sponsors and funding agencies that, over the years, have found theatre to be a meaningful enough part of our society to support it, and hope that their support grows and spreads across the country.

I would also like to thank all those who helped realize our most recent dream, *The Prithviwallahs*—Pramod Kapoor, Publisher, Roli Books for his belief in the relevance of this story, his team, Dipa Chaudhuri, Renuka Chatterjee and Sneha Pamneja for their invaluable inputs and eye for detail. And Deepa Gahlot for her patient effort in pulling the story out of us all and putting it together, Sucharita Apte for her detailed archiving work with all the visuals, and the photographers and archives whose visuals have made this book come alive, in particular Aditya Bhattacharya, Deepa Parekh, Hemant Chaturvedi, Meenal Agarwal, Narendra Shreshtha, Rajani Kapse, R.N. Kumtakar, Sidharth Siva, Suhas Khandke, Sangeet Natak Akademi, Tilakraj and Times Archives.

—Shashi Kapoor

Shashi Kapoor

presents

The Prithviwallahs

with

Deepa Gahlot

Lustre Press
Roli Books

'It goes on, I see, as my soul prompts it.'
—The Tempest

Scene I: Bombay

IT WAS THE WINTER OF 1928. THE Frontier Mail was flagged off from Peshawar—then still an integral part of pre-Partition India—on yet another routine journey to Bombay. For two days and two nights it snaked its way through the interminably rugged landscape that stretched from Peshawar to Bombay, before finally grinding to a halt at the railway terminus in Colaba where all inbound trains came to rest. The station, now long defunct, had none of the grandeur of the Victoria Terminus (present-day Shivaji Chhatrapati Terminus)—a recurrent backdrop in countless Indian films as a symbolic 'gateway' to India. Amongst the weary passengers who got off the train at this little terminal, was a strapping, strikingly handsome, 21-year-old man, carrying a suitcase in one hand and a hockey stick—his lucky charm—in the other. He was a stranger to the city that was yet to be rechristened Mumbai, but it was here that he had come to chase a dream.

Taking in his surroundings in a sweeping glance, the young man strode out of the station and summoned a Victoria (those quaint horse-drawn carriages that still ply in some parts of South Mumbai). He instructed the driver to take him to the seafront and a short while later, alighted at the Gateway of India. He looked at the shimmering sea stretching out before him, then raised his face to the heavens and said, 'Mr God, if you don't make me an actor and a star here, I will swim the seven seas and go to Hollywood.' That said, he asked the driver to take him to a hotel that was closest to a big film studio. The driver gave the young man a curious look. It was not often that he got such requests, and the young man in his Victoria seemed too aristocratic in his bearing to be a *filmwala*. Giving him a quick once over to gauge his financial worth, the driver decided to take him to Kashmir Hotel in front of Bombay's Metro cinema which cost Rs 5 a night. The hotel was a longish walk to Ardeshir Irani's Imperial Studio that had been set up at Kennedy Bridge just a couple of years earlier, at the height of the silent film era.

Kashmir Hotel, Prithviraj Kapoor's first abode in Bombay, still stands, though a little derelict; Metro is about to make way for a modern multiplex, and garages, offices and other nondescript businesses have now sprouted at the spot where Imperial Studio once stood.

Through 1927, Imperial Studio had had a run of successes—amongst them films like *Alibaba* and *Alladin*, directed by B.P. Mishra. The company boasted of a galaxy of stars: Sulochna, whose *Wild Cat of Bombay* was a big hit; Gauhar, who left to join Chandulal Shah's Kohinoor Studio, and went on to form a successful partnership with him at Ranjit

was thrilled to find a fellow Pathan with whom he could speak in his own language—Pushto. To chance upon something familiar in an alien land was reassuring and comforting. The watchman too was pleased to find a compatriot and immediately warmed to him. The two chatted for a while. The watchman tried hard to dissuade the young man from rushing headlong into the disreputable world of cinema, assuring him that only crazy people would ever want to be actors. But when he realized that nothing would shake this Pathan's resolve, he let him in, reluctantly wishing him well: 'If you are lucky, you will get work.'

On his first day in Bombay, the young Prithviraj Kapoor started his acting career standing in the line of extras who were picked up by production assistants on daily wages of Rs 2.50.

As luck would have it, on his third day at Imperial Studio, the main actor of *Cinema Girl*, a silent film under production, failed to turn up. A distraught and angry B.P. Mishra, the director of the film, decided to teach the truant a lesson. He asked the heroine Ermeline to pick an actor from the line of extras. Ermeline spotted Prithviraj Kapoor, looking every bit a Greek God, standing in the row of extras and beckoned to him.

PRITHVIRAJ KAPOOR WAS BORN ON 3 November 1906, in Peshawar, now in Pakistan. When he was three, his mother passed away, and his police officer father, Bashesharnath Kapoor, remarried. The child was sent to live with his grandfather in

Above: At Edwards College, Peshawar: (left to right) Hans (a friend), Principal Noble, Prithviraj Kapoor and Professor Jai Dayal.

Right: Professor Jai Dayal, Prithviraj Kapoor's mentor and friend.

Facing page: Rama Kapoor in Peshawar.

Movietone, and Ermeline, the beautiful Indian-Jewish actress, known as India's Clara Bow.

Cinema was still young, film companies were prospering and it was the right time to get into films.

At the gates of Imperial Studio, Prithviraj found his way barred by a burly Pathan watchman. Far from being disheartened, he

Samundri until he was old enough to return to Peshawar and live with his father.

When Prithviraj finished his schooling, Bashesharnath took him to meet Professor Jai Dayal, who taught at Peshawar's Edwards College, to consult him about the boy's future academic plans. Bashesharnath was keen on his son pursuing science, but Professor Dayal convinced him to let the young boy take up arts. The professor happened to be in charge of the dramatic society of Edwards College, and spotted talent immediately. Prithviraj was cast in the triple bill of one-act plays: *Dina Ki Baraat*, an original Punjabi play by R.L. Sahni, *Spreading the News* by Lady Gregory and *Riders to the Sea* by J.M. Synge. He first appeared on the college stage in the role of a woman to thunderous applause. The critics labelled his an outstanding performance. Prithviraj was hooked to acting.

In keeping with the custom of the times, Prithviraj Kapoor was married off at the age of 17, while still a student. Rama, his beautiful 14-year-old bride, had been orphaned as a child and brought up by neighbours. Prithviraj's heart was in acting but his father wanted him to study further. It wasn't easy to summon up the nerve to confront his father, who was as strict at home as he was as a police officer, so Prithviraj enrolled in law college. But his dilemma persisted till finally one day he found himself blurting out that he wanted to go to Bombay and become an actor. Needless to say, his father was furious. *'Kanjar banna hai?'* (Do you want to become a kanjar?) he fumed (Kanjars were a lowly

nomadic tribe of performers). But having once found the courage, Prithviraj was not going to give up so easily. He had the support of Kaushalya *bua*, his father's sister who was only a few years older than him. After his mother's death when he was just three, Kaushalya *bua* had looked after him and was sympathetic about his aspirations. So she gave him Rs 75 to pursue his dream. With that in his pocket, he sneaked off to Bombay, promising to send for his wife and three children later—of these, Raj Kapoor, born in 1924 in Peshawar, went on to become a cinema legend. The other two, Birendranath and Devendranath, died in infancy. Years later, Kaushalya *bua*'s son, Inderraj Anand would become a famous writer, and his son Tinu Anand, a well-known actor and filmmaker.

PRITHVIRAJ KAPOOR HAD COME TO Bombay knowing no one, and with no idea how to go about pursuing his dream. Getting a break at Imperial Studio in his very first week had indeed been a blessing. But in a city like Bombay, living in Kashmir Hotel was a drain on his pocket. He had to find another option before his dwindling funds dried up completely. So he set out to look for a room to rent when he got time off from shooting, and finally managed to find a place at Rs 20 a month, on the fourth floor of a dingy building in the heart of Bombay's red light area. The hero of *Cinema Girl* found himself living in the seamier part of Bombay, with Peshawar and the comforts of his father's home a distant dream. He had been there only a few days, when he hurt himself during

shooting. Laid up in bed with a swollen foot and high fever, he starved in his room for three days. On the fourth day, a young woman came to his room with a plate of food and shyly offered it to him.

She was afraid he would refuse to eat it because she was a prostitute who lived in the building across the road. She had noticed that the good-looking man had not left his room for three days, and had taken it upon herself to find out what had happened to him. To her amazement not only did Prithviraj eat the food gratefully, but also thanked her profusely for her kindness. The young woman looked after him till he recovered, and when finally he was well enough to resume shooting, he gave her a *rakhi* and held out his right hand to her. The tearful woman tied the homemade *rakhi* on his wrist. Through a strange quirk of fate,

CINEMA GIRL

Right: Prithviraj Kapoor with Ermeline in his first film *Cinema Girl* (1929).

Below: A still from Ardeshir Irani's *Alam Ara* (1931), India's first talkie, in which Prithviraj Kapoor played the heroine Zubeida's father.

Facing page: Prithviraj Kapoor as he looked in the early thirties.

they had sealed a bond in an equally strange city. Till she died, she tied a *rakhi* on Prithviraj's wrist every year.

The story is the stuff that many a Hindi film is made of, but it encapsulates an essential quality of the man. In the years to come, Prithviraj Kapoor, the star and director of his own touring repertory company, Prithvi Theatres, would never falter in generosity or kindness.

After *Cinema Girl*, Prithviraj went on to act in films like *Sher-e-Arab* (1930), *Vijay Kumar* (1930), *A Bid for the Throne* (1931), *A Wager in Love* (1931), *Toofan* (1931) and several silent films that achieved a measure of success. He also acted in India's first talkie, Ardeshir Irani's *Alam Ara* (1931)—the first 'all talking, singing, dancing picture'— with Master Vitthal and Zubeida. The characters in *Alam Ara* spoke colloquial Hindustani and sang seven songs. The film was a costume fantasy in which Prithviraj played the heroine's father.

Most actors, including *Alam Ara's* Master Vitthal had problems making the transition from silent films to talkies, because they did not have good voices. Prithviraj had the twin advantage of a theatre background and a rich voice, which he had taken the trouble to train and enhance, and his career thrived in the talkie era. But he was still not satisfied— he was not getting the kind of roles he wanted. He had had enough of costume dramas and action adventures—he yearned for roles that were closer to life.

By 1929, he had sent for his family from Peshawar. Shamsherraj 'Shammi' Kapoor was born in Bombay's Ajinkya Hospital the year

Alam Ara was released. This son too was fated to be a great film star.

Just when Prithviraj was beginning to get restless, the Grant Anderson Theatre Company arrived in India in 1930. Anderson was an English actor-manager who came to India with a few actors and technicians from England. He was keen to hire Indian actors, and for Prithviraj, this opened up new vistas. Back in Peshawar, Prithviraj had already acquired a firm grounding in Shakespearean theatre in Edward's College with his professors Jai Dayal and Nora Richards. So he joined the Grant Anderson company and started touring India with the troupe, winning great acclaim for his role of Laertes in *Hamlet*.

Years later, in an interview with a journalist, he had an amusing incident to relate about his short stint with this theatre company: 'When I played Mark Anthony the audience sat serious and breathless. With telling effect I managed to hold them, putting everything I had into the lines—"If you have tears, prepare to shed them, now." Unfortunately the word "now" synchronized, as if at a given signal, with the sudden howling of a child. After that, well it took quite some time to get the audience to stop laughing. It was too much for them.'

At around this time, he also played Charudutta in a production of Bhasa's Sanskrit classic, *Mrichhakatikam* (The Little Clay Cart), which Shashi Kapoor would turn into a film, *Utsav*, under his banner Film-valas almost half a century later, in 1985.

Prithviraj Kapoor was already a popular film star when he joined the theatre

company, but a small incident illustrates his dedication to his craft and his complete humility—a rare trait these days.

During a show in Delhi, he had a scene in which he had to drop dead. On cue, he tumbled and rolled to a spot where, a few seconds later, the heavy curtain, weighed down with a metal-lined border, was to come down. In a desperate stage whisper, a panic-stricken Anderson urged him, 'Move from there or the curtain will fall on your head.' Prithviraj lay still and did not move, and true enough, the curtain did roll down on his head. After the show was over, everyone rushed to see if he had been hurt. When Anderson admonished him for endangering himself, Prithviraj answered, 'Dead people don't move.'

Later Anderson said that had it been any other actor, he would have had to be hospitalized had the curtain hit him on the head. But Prithviraj was up and ready for the next show in no time.

In 1932, when they reached Calcutta, the Grant Anderson Theatre Company shut down. Anderson felt that he could not carry on any longer, and decided to retire from the stage. But for Prithviraj, being in the city proved useful—he joined New Theatres and acted in some of the best films of his career—*Rajrani Meera* (1933), *Seeta* (1934), *Manzil* (1936), *President* (1937) and the classic *Vidyapathi* (1937) where he played King Shiva Singha whose wife falls in love with the poet Vidyapathi.

In Calcutta his family grew—daughter Urmila was born in 1933, and his youngest son Shashi Kapoor in 1938. By this time, Prithviraj's father, stepmother and seven half brothers and sisters—Trilok (who later became a fairly well-known film actor), Kaushalya, Amar, Prem, Ram, Shanta and Vishi—had joined him at the two-storey house at Hazra Road, Kalighat, next to the fire station. Prithviraj looked after the entire clan—their education, upkeep, marriage were his responsibility. Such was his sense of duty towards his family that Shashi and Urmila were born at home, because at that time he was paying for the deliveries of his sisters, and could not bear additional hospital expenses for his own wife.

After about seven years in Calcutta, the Kapoors moved back to Bombay in 1939. In those days, actors were employed by studios on a monthly salary, and after a while Prithviraj started getting frustrated. He felt that New Theatres gave preference to Bengali actors and technicians. For the next two years, Prithviraj worked with old associate Chandulal Shah's Ranjit Movietone in films like *Aaj Ka Hindustan* (1940) and *Paagal* (1940).

Prithviraj was the first star who bucked the studio system that employed actors exclusively on a monthly salary. He felt that his talents were not being fully utilized as long as he was restricted to working with a single studio, so he started the 'freelance' contract system. Being a freelance actor gave him the freedom to choose better and more varied roles—and by then he was such a big name that he faced no resistance. His 'rebellion' was one of the factors that ultimately brought down the all-powerful studio autocracy.

The most memorable film of his career was yet to come. The title role in the legendary actor-producer-director Sohrab Modi's *Sikander* (1941) immortalized Prithviraj Kapoor. This epic film was set in 326 B.C. when Alexander the Great, having conquered Persia and the Kabul Valley, reaches the Indian border and encounters resistance from King Porus. As Alexander the Great in the film, Prithviraj would meet his match in King Porus, played by Sohrab Modi.

When Modi narrated the subject to Prithviraj and signed him for the role, he asked him, 'What will be your contribution to the character?' Prithviraj went home, pondered over the question, and made a decision. He sent his family back to Peshawar, and for three months worked single-mindedly on building his body and fleshing out the character in his mind. It was his idea to turn Alexander into an impish character, and give him the affable gesture of slapping his thigh.

By the time the film went on the floor, Prithviraj 'became' Alexander. He so embodied the character that history textbooks started printing his picture as Alexander the Great. Shashi Kapoor, who was then studying at Don Bosco school,

remembers feeling embarrassed yet more than a little proud when he came across his father's picture in class.

One day, while the shooting of *Sikandar* was on, and Prithviraj was in costume, he did not stand up when Modi entered the set, as was customary, nor did he wish Modi. When Modi asked him why he had not greeted him, Prithviraj replied, 'Sikandar does not know Sohrab Modi.' Modi saluted his Sikander and said, 'But I know Sikandar.'

Though the exceedingly hospitable

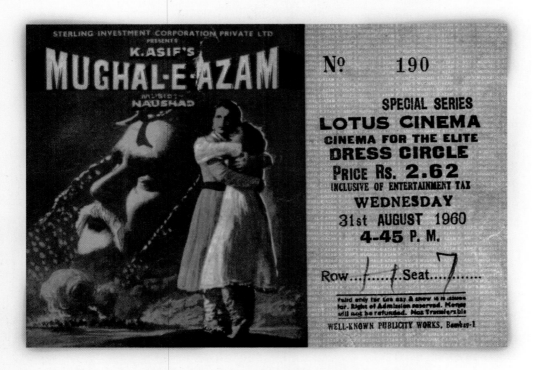

Had he turned to theatre at any other time of his life, he would have been accused of using it to cover up for his failure in films. But it was a genuine love for theatre that drove him back to the stage that year.

Kapoor household was always overflowing with people, Sohrab Modi was the only film personality who was accorded the honour of a formal dinner at Prithviraj's house, after he got married to actress Mehtaab.

The same year, Prithviraj Kapoor starred opposite Sadhana Bose in one of the earliest 'crossover' films made for an international market, J.B.H. Wadia's lavish and ambitious English-Hindi-Bengali production, *Court Dancer.*

Besides *Sikandar,* Prithviraj's other most memorable role was in a historical, *Mughal-e-Azam* (1960) in which he played Emperor

Akbar to perfection—with impeccable regal carriage and an authoritative, booming voice that underlined the emperor's hauteur. But this would also put unimaginable strain on the actor's voice with serious repercussions on his health and career.

In 1944, though, Prithviraj, having already tasted success with *Sikandar*, was at his peak, and felt drawn to theatre once again. Had he turned to theatre at any other time of his life, he would have been accused of using it to cover up for his failure in films. But it was a genuine love for theatre that drove him back to the stage that year.

Scene II: Prithvi Theatres is Born

IT WAS THE JANUARY OF 1944. IN the mild chill of a late winter night in Bombay, Prithviraj Kapoor paced up and down College Road, Matunga, where he lived. An idea had been brewing in his mind for sometime now. He walked for some more time, then stubbed out his cigarette, went home and declared to Rama that he was going to set up a theatre company. The remuneration from theatre would obviously be negligible compared to his income from films—the implication being that she was to brace herself to face some hard times.

Having married Prithviraj in her early teens, Rama was by then completely assimilated into the Kapoor household. Such was her unshakeable faith in her husband and children that she firmly believed they could do no wrong, and would agree to anything her husband asked of her. Dare

Above: Prithvi Theatres on tour in Ahmedabad. Prithviraj Kapoor is seen with his wife Rama and young son Shashi. To his right (in black), is his cousin and Prithvi Theatres' manager Nandkishore Kapoor.

Facing page: Prithvi Theatres on tour in Bihar. Seen in the picture are Prithviraj Kapoor's father Bashesharnath Kapoor (with a gray moustache). On the extreme right is Prithviraj Kapoor's aunt Kaushalya (Buaji), who supported and financed his move to Bombay to join films.

anyone criticize her husband or children even jokingly in her presence, and the gentle woman would transform into a tigress. Like women of that generation, she never addressed him by name. He was always 'Woh.'

She had never questioned his earlier decision to leave Peshawar for Bombay. She had not questioned his decision to send the family back from Bombay to Peshawar when he was preparing for *Sikandar*. Now, when he

told her of his decision to start a theatre company, she accepted it stoically once again even though it meant she would be separated from him for long periods of time, or, if she travelled with him, go through all the discomforts and travails of life in a touring theatre.

Sometimes, when a man is determined, even fate conspires to be on his side. Prithviraj believed that, 'Nature determines the right moment for everything.'

A friend of his, Pandit Narayan Prasad 'Betaab', had written a play, Shakuntala based on Kalidasa's famous classic. For some reason the organization that was to produce the play backed out. So Prithviraj decided that the first home production of Prithvi Theatres would be Shakuntala. Betaab, a famous writer who had written several film scripts for Ranjit Movietone, was considered to be of the same stature as the most popular playwright of the time—Agha Hashr Kashmiri. To produce his play would be a coup for Prithvi Theatres.

On 15 January 1944, Prithvi Theatres formally came into being. A havan was performed on the auspicious occasion at Dhuru Hall in Dadar, very close to Chhabildas Hall, where years later Mumbai's experimental theatre would bloom. The Kapoor clan dressed in white churidar kurtas had turned up in full force. Amidst the chanting of hymns, the fragrant air was charged with the excitement of a dream breaking free of its cocoon. Nobody could have known then that this moment was to mark the beginning of many undying friendships and loyal relationships, of bonhomie and outstanding careers, and of a nomadic way of life that would be as tough as it would be fulfilling.

Raj Kapoor, who was about 19 years old when Prithvi Theatres took birth, had assisted director Kidar Sharma for a while, and had also signed on a couple of films as

Shakuntala: 1944, First Production of Prithvi Theatres

Left: Prithviraj Kapoor as Dushyant and Uzra Mumtaz as Shakuntala in the play.

Above: B.M. Vyas and Uzra Mumtaz playing Rishi Kanva and Shakuntala. Vyas joined the film industry and acted in several mythological films.

Facing page: Kashinath Bhatt (below) played the Vidushak. Prithviraj Kapoor as Dushyant with son Shashi Kapoor as Bharat (above) in the play. Shashi took over the role after brother Shammi outgrew the part.

an actor. He was given the responsibility of stage manager, and was put in charge of costumes, hair, make-up, lights, sets, sound and music for *Shakuntala*. Though he had no training in these departments, young Raj had a fine aesthetic sense. The sets were constructed in Dhuru Hall, the costumes were stitched on the terrace of the Kapoor residence, and soon it was time to begin casting.

Three people came from Hyderabad to audition for *Shakuntala* and, if possible, work with Prithvi Theatres. Two were selected, but they said either they all stayed, or they all went. So Prithviraj took on all three. They were Satyanarayan, who went on to become

a famous choreographer in films; Hemavati, who later married actor Sapru, and gave birth to actors Tej, Preeti and writer-director Reema; the third was Shankar, who later teamed up with Jaikishen to form a legendary and long-running partnership and composed some of the finest songs heard in Hindi films—many of them for Raj Kapoor.

When Prithviraj was with New Theatres in Calcutta, he had befriended sitar player Ram Ganguly, and promised him that if he ever made a film or play, he would invite Ganguly to score the music. He kept the promise, and Ganguly and his group of musicians were invited to Bombay to do the music for *Shakuntala*. Later, Ganguly

composed the music for Raj Kapoor's first film *Aag*.

Rehearsals for *Shakuntala* began, but there was still no Shakuntala in sight. Film actresses Vanmala and Swarnlata were considered for the role. The latter even came to rehearse, but begged off at the end of the very first day as it was too exhausting for her.

Prithviraj had heard of an actress called Damyanti (later to be actor Balraj Sahni's wife and actor Parikshit Sahni's mother) who was working in a K.A. Abbas play *Zubeida* for the Indian People's Theatre Association (IPTA) at the Cowasjee Jehangir Hall, now the National Gallery of Modern Art. He went to

combines qualities rarely to be found coupled—she is both emotional and intellectual. Though there is a dreaminess about her and in her speech a faint lisp, she is level-headed, has a straight back and a well-poised carriage. By no means goody-goody, she is good, and her friendships are deep and abiding as are most friendships of men. There is, in fact, something rather manly about her in spite of her charming femininity. She is rationalistic in outlook so her words are well weighed, not over talkative in society, as are so many emancipated Indian women.'

After *Shakuntala*, Uzra became a permanent actress with Prithvi Theatres, and went on to do the female lead in all productions except *Ahoothi*. Over the years, many of Prithvi's actors and actresses left to get into films, but Uzra remained with the theatre till it closed down in 1960. Zohra Segal too was to join Prithvi Theatres later, as dance director, and also acted in many plays.

K.N. Singh, the well-known film actor and a friend of Prithviraj, was initially cast as Rishi Kanva, who headed the ashram where Shakuntala was raised. But the actor had trouble with Sanskrit shlokas, so B.M. Vyas, who had come from Rajasthan to be a singer, stepped into the role, and intoned the shlokas with Brahminical precision.

Prithviraj's family gave him more than just moral support for his first production. While Raj managed affairs backstage, Shammi, then a student at Don Bosco school, played Bharat—Shakuntala and Raja Dushyant's son. Since the show would get over quite late, he would invariably be drowsy at school the next morning. One day, the principal summoned Prithviraj to the school. Elder brother Raj arrived for the appointment instead. The principal spelt out his decision clearly: 'Either the boy attends school or he does theatre.' Without a moment's hesitation, Raj said he would rather his brother became an actor, and promptly withdrew him from the school. Shammi was then admitted to New Era school, from where ultimately he did his matriculation. The principal of this school was Mrs Vyas, whose granddaughter is now a famous table player, Anuradha Pal.

Prithviraj's youngest son Shashi, acted in a crowd scene in *Shakuntala*, throwing himself wholeheartedly into the role, then graduated to playing Bharat when elder brother Shammi grew out of the role.

After arduous rehearsals, *Shakuntala* opened on 9 March 1945 at the Royal Opera House, and was hugely appreciated.

In fact, if the truth be told, Prithviraj had had another reason for selecting *Shakuntala* as Prithvi Theatres' first production. V. Shantaram was making a film on Shakuntala around the same time. It was taken for granted that Prithviraj Kapoor would play King Dushyant. Who else in the industry had the regal looks and the well-toned body needed to play a king? It came as a shock to Prithviraj when V. Shantaram signed up Chandramohan for the role. So Prithviraj decided to produce the stage version of *Shakuntala* and play the character of Raja Dushyant himself.

see the play, to see if Damyanti was right for the role. There he met another actress Uzra Mumtaz, younger sister of Zohra Segal—and knew he had found his Shakuntala.

Uzra Mumtaz, who now lives in Pakistan, and still acts in an occasional play, recalls, 'I can't say what attracted Prithviraj Kapoor to me or why he preferred me for the role of Shakuntala. He didn't say anything. After landing up a few times at the hall where we were rehearsing for *Zubeida*, he used to send me the car and say, "Please come and watch my rehearsals." Then after some time he selected me.'

Professor Jai Dayal writes in his book, *I Go South with Prithvi Theatres:* 'Uzra

Later, when the film was screened, the critics predictably compared the two Raja Dushyants. The magazine *Film India* reported, 'Stage *Shakuntala* beats film *Shakuntala*.' This was quite a compliment coming from Baburao Patel, the usually acerbic editor and film critic of the magazine, whose irrational aversion for Prithviraj Kapoor was no secret in the Bombay film world.

Despite being appreciated, *Shakuntala* was such an expensive production, that it ran into a financial loss of nearly Rs 1 lakh. Shashi ,who took over as stage manager when he was older, recalls the heavy wagonloads of *Shakuntala* sets that were 'hell to assemble and dismantle'. The show had to be discontinued after some years for this reason. But to celebrate the first show at Prithvi Theatres, Prithviraj paid a bonus of two months' salary to the entire cast and management from his own pocket.

Between 1944 and '45, Prithviraj's cousins Kamal and Ravinder Kapoor joined the theatre; so did cousins Premnath and Rajindernath, Sajjan and Mohan Saigal—all of whom gained fame in films; sisters Kumud and Indumati who went on to join the Sachin Shanker Ballet Troupe, and actress Pushpa, who married actor and scriptwriter Prayag Raj—Raj himself had joined Prithvi Theatres as a child. Two more cousins Nand Kishore Kapoor and Pran Nath Khanna took over the managerial reins. Then there was Satidevi who was the sister of Satyajit Ray's wife Bijoya, and mother of Kishore Kumar's first wife Ruma; L.V. Prasad, who went on to set up his own film empire in Chennai, and

Sardar Malik whose son Anu is a popular music director now.

Zohra Segal says, perhaps in jest, that Prithviraj Kapoor could never say 'no' to anyone who came to join Prithvi Theatres. He made place for everybody in the group, and paid everybody a fair salary each month. More often than not the salaries were paid out of his earnings from films. Once he even allowed a dacoit named Jaggi to join the troupe. Jaggi was a good singer, but the girls were terrified of him, and he eventually had to leave. Prithviraj introduced him to Dara Singh the wrestler and stunt film star, and the dacoit did go on to act in quite a few Dara Singh films!

Prayag Raj recalls coming to Mumbai with his mother and infant brother following the death of his father, who had told the nine-year-old child, 'If anything should happen to me, go to Papaji.'

Prithviraj Kapoor was 'Papaji' to the whole industry. He came to acquire that name thanks to his son Raj who could not pronounce 'Bhapaji'—the Punjabi word for elder brother. Little Raj had always heard everyone call his father 'Bhapaji' and thought that was what he too was supposed to call him. But 'Bhapaji' came out as 'Papaji' from the child's mouth and soon, Prithviraj Kapoor was affectionately called 'Papaji' by everyone.

It was Papaji's custom to empty out his pockets for the line of supplicants who would gather outside his house each morning, waiting for him to emerge. Feeling a trifle lost and nervous, little Prayag Raj joined the queue. As he went down the line

that morning, Papaji suddenly felt a tug at his kurta. He looked down to see a child staring up at him, hope and expectation writ large on his face. Prayag told him who he was, and why he had come—he needed a job. Papaji stood and listened intently to the child, a smile on his face, as he leaned back on the black Opel in which he drove to work. Without much ado, he told Prayag to join the troupe and report for work at the Royal Opera House at 9 a.m. the next morning. Prayag thanked Papaji, started walking away, then turned around and asked, 'How much will you pay me?' A startled Papaji laughed and replied, '25 rupees.'

So a nine-year-old joined the troupe on a salary, appeared in crowd scenes in *Shakuntala* and played the role of Bharat when Shammi was too old for it, and Shashi could not tour with the troupe when school terms were on.

The black Opel, a 1939 model, was the car that Prithviraj had bought with his first earnings and he did not replace it for a long time. Years later, when Raj Kapoor became a star and filmmaker, he gave his father a blank cheque for a car. Papaji wrote 'with love' on it and kept it. He would show the cheque proudly to friends—a sign of his famous son's love. It was only sometime at the end of the '50s that he bought himself a Standard Herald, which he drove himself.

Harikishen 'Tiger' Kapoor, another cousin impressed by Papaji, expressed the desire to join Prithvi Theatres. For a year or so, he was just made to watch rehearsals and observe performances from the wings. 'After a year and a half he asked me whether I got paid.

Prithviraj Kapoor recording a Prithvi
Theatres play at the All India Radio studio.

When I said no, he fixed a salary of Rs 25 a month. After two years, I got a small role of a cloth seller in a play. My voice was too thin, so Papaji suggested I go to the seaside and shout. "That will help develop your voice," he told me.

'By then, I felt I had learnt every role. It seemed as though Papaji was simply ignoring me. Then suddenly everything changed. We were in Agra for our shows and it was 2.30 at night, when I was on my way to the loo. He came up to me from behind and said I

Prithviraj Kapoor with his beloved Opel which he never gave up. It used to be parked behind Prithvi Theatre in Juhu, till the mid-eighties.

Facing page: Prithviraj Kapoor during his stint as a member of the Sangeet Natak Akademi and Member of Parliament.

was to be on stage the next evening in *Pathan*. The moment that I had waited for was finally here, but I was petrified. The following day I prayed before going on stage. After the show, he hugged me and said, "I was ignoring you so that the fire burns inside you. That has happened now." He had succeeded in raising a *toofan* (storm) in me.

'Sometimes people asked him if there was a method that he used. Perhaps he had a method of his own, but I can't really say much. He had never studied acting. He would often say, "*10 janam chahiye, mujhe to ek janam poora nahin hua.*" ' (You need ten births to perfect the art, I have yet to complete my first.)

Geoffrey Kendal, who ran his own theatre company Shakespeareana, and who was to later become Prithviraj's samdhi (his daughter Jennifer married Shashi Kapoor), writes in his book *The Shakespearewallahs*, 'Prithviraj was a throwback to the old-time English actor-managers. He loved it all— being a father figure, a great actor, the idol of all and sundry. He did everything in a big way and he acted all the time, on stage and off, but he was genuinely good-hearted and unbelievably kind to his company. He spent much of what he earned in films to keep his theatre troupe together out of pure charity.'

At the time Prithviraj Kapoor set up Prithvi Theatres, 'in a theatreless land' as Nora Richards wrote in her Preface to *I Go South*, there was no professional Hindi repertory company. There were only a handful of small travelling folk theatre groups, and some Parsi theatre, performing the works of Agha Hashr Kashmiri.

Prithvi Theatres gave Hindustani theatre its rightful place in the sun.

PRITHVIRAJ KAPOOR INTRODUCED A naturalistic style of acting, perhaps inspired by the Hollywood films that he watched avidly at the cinema whenever he got the chance. His plays were realistic; there was no coming down to the footlights to address the audience. He was the first man in Hindi theatre to stand with his back to the audience, then speak and yet be heard, through the powerful projection of his voice; emote and be understood through the sheer strength of his performance. He broke the conventions of Corinthian theatre prevalent then.

Parsi theatre—the most popular manifestation of Corinthian Theatre— was undoubtedly very popular with the audience, and continues to exercise, to this day, an important influence on our mainstream cinema. The structure of Parsi theatre, with its songs, comedy track, even 'item' numbers is the one most mainstream films continue to follow. Faredoon Irani, father of actress Aroona Irani and director Indra Kumar, had a famous Parsi theatre company, where some of today's stage stars like Sarita Joshi, cut their teeth. But the audience was ready for a change and Prithvi Theatres provided it.

As a child, Prithviraj had gone with his father to see a performance of *Harishchandra Taramati*. In one scene, a mother picked up her dead child and sang a song in a tearful voice. At the end of the song, the audience collectively chanted 'once more, once more'. The woman put the child down on stage, picked it up, and sang the song again. Shaukat Kaifi remembers Papaji telling the group later, 'My little heart said, this is wrong, she should not have sung again. I have rescued this theatre from the influence of the Corinthian Theatre.'

He read a lot of English theatre biographies and admired John Gielgud, over the more popular Lawrence Olivier. He thought Gielgud's voice was very good and that he was honest to the text and faithful to the playwright while Olivier was more sensational. Prithviraj was a strong advocate of realism and believed in the words of one of the most famous English actors of his time, who was also the first to be knighted—Sir Henry Irving: 'In the consideration of the art of acting, it must never be forgotten that the ultimate aim is beauty.'

After *Shakuntala*, Prithviraj Kapoor decided to do only original plays commissioned by him. He wanted to do plays that were socially relevant and close to reality. Communal tensions and impending Partition offered him the material for the kind of patriotic, social plays that he wanted to do. Prithvi Theatres did seven plays after *Shakuntala* —*Deewar* (1945), *Pathan* (1947), *Ghaddar* (1948), *Ahoothi* (1949), *Kalakar* (1951), *Paisa* (1953) and *Kisan* (1956). All of them took up powerful, contemporary themes.

Scene III: The Plays

GEOFFREY KENDAL ONCE said, 'Being an actor must be the best job in the world. It combines all the things that a person need look for: health, romance, travel, the fun of the lottery, the positive tragedy of failure and the will to overcome it . . . good companionship.'

Prithviraj Kapoor too had the best job in the world and all that went with it. Prithvi Theatres was a completely self-sufficient theatre. The number of permanent salaried staff was about 100, which swelled to 150 including actors, playwrights, carpenters, electricians, make-up and costume men, cooks, managers, booking clerks, travel arrangers, when the company went on tour. All it needed was an audience—and that, for a star of Prithviraj's standing, was not too difficult to get.

Prithviraj did not encourage dilettantism. At Prithvi Theatres, rehearsals were on every day, from 11 a.m. to 2 p.m. when the troupe was on tour and from 10 a.m. to 2 p.m. when they were back in Bombay. This routine was strictly followed, even when there was no play to rehearse. At such times, Prithviraj would simply hold a 'class', and speak on philosophy and other subjects.

In keeping with the tradition of Western repertory companies, Prithvi Theatres had a uniquely democratic system—everybody was treated alike. On stage, only Prithviraj played the main roles and had no understudy. Everyone else played all the other parts—an actor could be a hero one day, and an extra the next. Since all the actors were present at the rehearsals, everybody automatically ended up learning all the parts and could take on any role in any play at short notice.

Shashi Kapoor remembers the Max Factor make-up the actors and actresses used. This was a departure from the 'typical theatrical make-up which was cheap and bad for the skin which was used by many *nautanki* companies. I came to know more about make-up when I joined Shakespeareana in 1957. I discovered there was a German company, Lichner, which specialized in theatre make-up, and even the British and American companies used that. That was very good. The audience starts at 15 yards from the stage, so you have to project not only your voice but also your acting and make-up. The make-up need not look so nice at close range but it has to be seen with the lights, from 15 yards away. Since most of Prithvi Theatres' plays were modern except *Shakuntala*, there was very little use of make-up.

'Wigs were made in-house, because we could not afford to buy them. Shyam Kansare and Narendranath Grover were the wig-makers. Shyam had come to Prithvi Theatres in his teens, and grew up with us because his brother-in-law Madhav Pai was one of the chief make-up men at Prithvi Theatres, and later with RK Studios. More Dada and Madhav Dada were the other make-up people.'

Papaji never actually 'trained' anyone. He always said, 'I am not a teacher, don't treat me as a guru.' At Prithvi Theatres, everybody learnt through observation and instinct, honed by long hours of watching their seniors rehearse or perform.

After some years on the road, Papaji felt the time had come for him to have an understudy. He decided to experiment with Ramesh Saigal, the chief assistant director, and asked him to study the role of Dushyant in *Shakuntala*. (Saigal went on to become a well-known film producer, and director of films like *Shaheed, Phir Subah Hogi, Railway Platform*). The whole play was performed with Saigal playing Dushyant opposite Damyanti Sahni as Shakuntala, while Prithviraj sat in the audience and watched him. When the curtain fell, the opinion was unanimous—only Prithviraj could play the part. So Prithviraj continued to play the lead roles in all Prithvi productions and there was no further talk about getting an understudy for him.

For tours, a third class train-bogey would be booked and everyone would travel in it, including Prithviraj. The one thing that Prithviraj achieved during his stint as a Rajya Sabha member from 1952 to 1959, was to get a 75 per cent rail concession for performing artists. Artists avail of this concession till date. His contention was that performing artists, be they actors or circus folk, often slashed their fees or made other sacrifices to reach the average Indian audience. The least the government could do was subsidize their travel expenses. As

The Prithvi Theatres troupe at the Delhi station after a tour of Kashmir in 1952. **(Left to right):** B.M. Vyas (with sunglasses), Chandramuni, Vishwa Mehra (Mamaji), Ismail, Mrs Rama Kapoor, Pyarelal (Prithviraj's valet), Prithviraj, Kuku Khanna, Bashesharnath Kapoor (Bade Papaji), two unidentified troupe members, Banke Bihari aka Rochak Pandit (who produced Mani Kaul's first film *Uski Roti*), Harikishen 'Tiger' Kapoor and Rajan Kapoor(seated).

an MP, Prithviraj had the option of flying or travelling first class, but he preferred to be with the troupe. Premnath once wrote in a piece on him, 'He scolded Raj and me whenever we took it easy reminding us we were not *jagirdars* (landowners) but *mazdoors* (labourers).'

He disliked silks and synthetics, and always wore white khadi or cotton, ate when someone served him food and slept on the floor. Nobody remembers him ever complaining of discomfort.

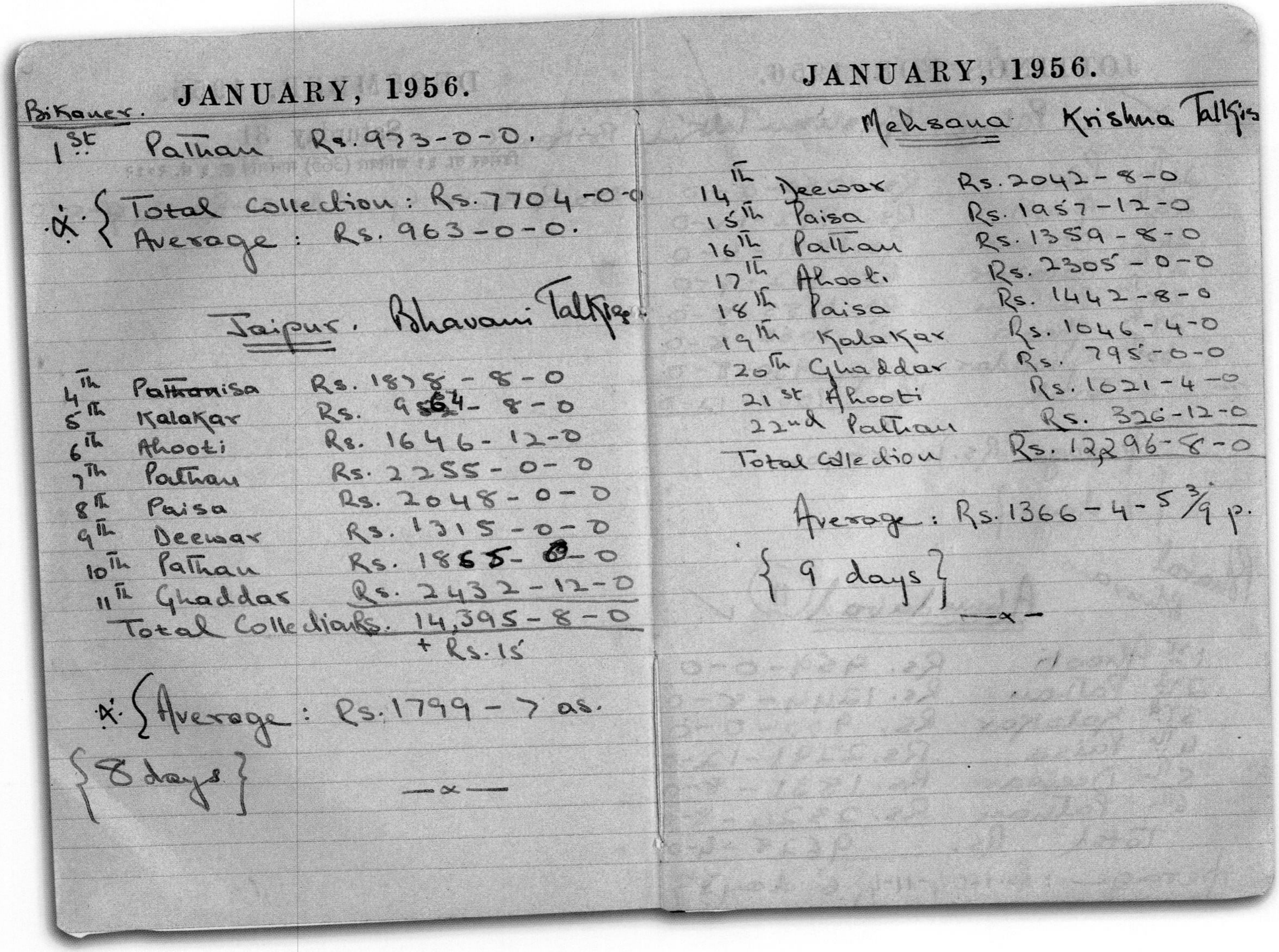

Bikaner.

1st Pathan Rs. 973-0-0.

∴ { Total Collection : Rs. 7704-0-0
     Average : Rs. 963-0-0.

Jaipur. Bhavani Talkies.

4th	Pathanisa	Rs. 1878-8-0
5th	Kalakar	Rs. 964-8-0
6th	Ahooti	Rs. 1646-12-0
7th	Pathan	Rs. 2255-0-0
8th	Paisa	Rs. 2048-0-0
9th	Deewar	Rs. 1315-0-0
10th	Pathan	Rs. 1855-0-0
11th	Ghaddar	Rs. 2432-12-0
	Total Collections.	14,395-8-0
		+ Rs. 15

∴ { Average : Rs. 1799 - 7 as.

{ 8 days }

— x —

Mehsana   Krishna Talkies

14th	Deewar	Rs. 2042-8-0
15th	Paisa	Rs. 1957-12-0
16th	Pathan	Rs. 1359-8-0
17th	Ahooti	Rs. 2305-0-0
18th	Paisa	Rs. 1442-8-0
19th	Kalakar	Rs. 1046-4-0
20th	Ghaddar	Rs. 795-0-0
21st	Ahooti	Rs. 1021-4-0
22nd	Pathan	Rs. 326-12-0
	Total Collection	Rs. 12,296-8-0

Average : Rs. 1366-4-5 3/9 p.

{ 9 days }

— x —

Shaukat Kaifi, remembers going to meet him and standing up as a mark of respect, when he walked into the room. At this Prithviraj smiled and said, 'Anyone who stands up for me is fined one anna.'

All through the year, Prithvi Theatres remained on the move, performing in small towns all over the country and staying in small lodges or rented bungalows. Once, in Sangli, they even stayed in a *gowshala* (cowshed). 'We never stayed in hotels,' recalls Shashi Kapoor. 'We could not afford it.

'Shri Prithviraj Kapoor has done great service to the Indian theatre. He was a Member of the Rajya Sabha and was always listened to with great attention. Whenever tensions ran high, he made soothing speeches.'

S. RADHAKRISHNAN
Vice-President, India

Ten rupees was the highest ticket rate, so the overall income was not really much. Everybody carried their hold-alls and trunks and slept on the floor. My father had a very small room to himself. There used to be a kind of assembly hall in each town where we would have our rehearsals. If the theatre where we were supposed to perform was nearby, then we rehearsed in the theatre.'

The troupe's arrival in a small town always created a lot of excitement. People were awestruck by the presence of Prithviraj

Kapoor, the film star, in their town. Tongas and rickshaws were willingly pressed into service in the streets for public announcements of the performances.

Most cities did not have proper theatres in those days, so cinema halls were converted into makeshift stages. A team was sent in advance to make alterations in the halls and earmark a big enough performing area. Carpenters would remove the first five or six rows and extend the stage with a makeshift platform jutting out. Another

Facing page: Pages from Shashi Kapoor's diary, in which he entered the daily collections of Prithvi Theatres. Shashi was assistant stage manager at that time.

Below: Prithviraj Kapoor at the Executive Board meeting of the Sangeet Natak Akademi. Seen on the left in dark glasses is the legendary dancer Uday Shankar, elder brother of sitar maestro Pandit Ravi Shankar.

problem was that cinema halls were not equipped with wings at the sides, so many a time, walls had to be broken down to construct temporary wings and reconstructed after the show.

'That was the main reason,' says Shashi Kapoor, 'why Papaji wanted proper theatres in the country.' The government had appointed him on the committee set up to establish Rabindra Natya Mandirs in many cities. In the beginning, when the first 10-15 theatres were built, he was quite excited. But

he soon realized that most people on the committee had no idea about the requirements of performers. Even today most theatres are not quite user-friendly. When Shashi and Jennifer Kapoor built the Prithvi Theatre in Prithviraj's memory, despite a space crunch, the comforts of the performing group and the audience were foremost on their minds.

Shimla's Gaiety Theatre, a beautiful hall with a compact Elizabethan stage, balconies and boxes was one venue that was a delight to perform in. Coincidentally, Ved Segan, the architect who designed Prithvi Theatre in Juhu is in charge of renovating Gaiety in Shimla. Shashi Kapoor vividly remembers the shooting of the Merchant-Ivory film *Shakespearewallah* (1964) at Gaiety Theatre. His own grounding in theatre first with Prithvi Theatres, then with Shakespeareana came in handy when he helped cinematographer Subrata Mitra do the lighting since he did not really know much about stage lighting or how Shakespearean theatre worked.

Each time the troupe travelled during school vacations, the younger children, Shammi, Urmila and Shashi, accompanied Prithviraj. Rama Kapoor had long accepted the fact that he loved theatre and needed to travel with his troupe. Whenever she could, she would accompany him. Rumours of his affairs with other women were legion. A man that handsome was bound to attract women like a magnet. But due to the absence of film gossip magazines in those days, these rumours never crossed the rubicon of backstage gossip.

Prithviraj was fiercely protective of the ladies working in the troupe. In some

Above: Prithviraj Kapoor and wife Rama in a relaxed mood at Raj Kapoor's house in Chembur. Raj Kapoor had bought the piano for his eldest daughter Ritu.

Facing page: Prithviraj Kapoor in a cheerful mood.

conservative towns, men tended to pass crude remarks at the actresses. Prithviraj did not shy away from admonishing the eve-teasers, or even attacking them to defend the actresses. He made no distinction between the actresses in the troupe and female members of his own family. Once, in Hyderabad, when a man made a vulgar jest, Prithviraj was so angry that he lifted the man in the air along with his bicycle and threw him down on the ground.

Prithvi Theatres managed without luxuries that people take for granted today. The places where they performed were not air-conditioned, neither did they have comfortable green rooms, or proper acoustics for that matter. Everyone washed their own clothes and utensils, and ate the

Prithvi Theatres: A Labour of Love

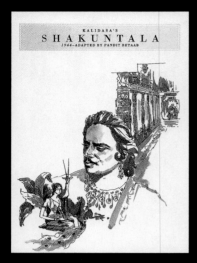

Shakuntala
OPENED: 9 March 1944
TOTAL SHOWS: 212

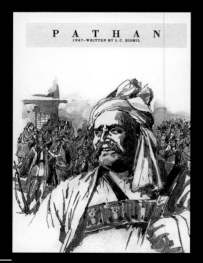

Pathan
OPENED: 13 April 1947
TOTAL SHOWS: 558

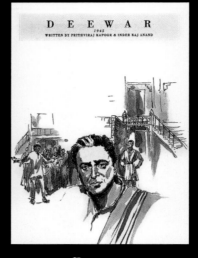

Deewar
OPENED: 9 August 1945
TOTAL SHOWS: 712

Ghaddar
OPENED: 15 August 1948
TOTAL SHOWS: 262

Shakuntala was based on Kalidasa's classic mythological love-story between King Dushyant and Shakuntala.

Deewar predicted Partition and explored the effect of the 'foreign' hand in dividing a close-knit family.

Pathan evoked the culture, tradition, loyalty, honour and sacrifice of the northwest frontier region, through the story of a Hindu and a Muslim Pathan family.

Ghaddar portrayed a man's disillusionment with politics and was set between the 1920s and Independence.

AHOOTHI
1949—WRITTEN BY L.C. BISMIL

KALAKAR
1952
WRITTEN BY RAMANAND SAGAR & PRITHVIRAJ KAPOOR

Total Shows Performed:
2662
2662 performances in 5982 days.
Paisa has been filmed.
Deewar and *Pathan* have been
recorded by Premnath.
Deewar and *Pathan* have been
translated in Russian.

Ahoothi
OPENED: 30 September 1949
TOTAL SHOWS: 339

Kalakar
OPENED: 8 September 1951
TOTAL SHOWS: 157

PAISA
1954—WRITTEN BY L.C. BISMIL

KISAN
1956—WRITTEN BY SHEELJI

Paisa
OPENED: 4 September 1953
TOTAL SHOWS: 302

Kisan
OPENED: 26 October 1956
TOTAL SHOWS: 120

Ahoothi dealt with the sufferings of an Indian family during Partition and their traumatic journey from Rawalpindi to Bombay.

Kalakar reaffirmed that beauty has its own place in nature through an artist's love for a village belle and her transformation in the city.

Paisa was Prithvi Theatres' most popular play about what money can do to a middle- class family.

Kisan presented Gandhiji's views of the Indian farmer and the effect of modernization on his life.

same food that was simple but plentiful. Whenever Rama Kapoor accompanied the troupe, she arranged a high tea before each performance. Otherwise it was tea and Monaco biscuits, and *pedas* after the show.

Shaukat Kaifi says that mealtimes after the shows were noisy and chaotic affairs, with everybody demanding different types of rotis—soft, extra crisp and so on. There were fights with the cooks over the way eggs were to be cooked. Those who wanted their fried eggs sunny side up would throw a fit if the yolk was broken. Once when some actors were making a fuss over the eggs, Papaji was watching. He called out to the cook and said, 'All those eggs these people have thrown away…make a big omelette and give it to me.'

Zohra Segal remembers that breakfast used to be two eggs, toast and tea for everyone, including the servants who travelled with the actors. Many of the actors couldn't afford to give their servants such luxuries when they were back home in Bombay. So Zohra, Uzra and Satidevi approached Prithviraj and spoke to him about the problem. Prithviraj promptly replied, 'Okay, I will stop the eggs for the three of you'—a response that typified both his sense of humour as well as his democratic attitude.

Leading such a large and diverse troupe must have been strenuous, but nobody recalls Prithviraj ever losing his composure. He did get angry once in a while, and ticked off people, but mildly. His favourite cusswords were *bhoot* (ghost), *gadha* (ass) and *ullu ka pattha* (son of an owl).

In her book *Stages* Zohra Segal writes, 'Before starting rehearsals each play was read to the entire cast and company technicians, inviting suggestions and criticism. Except for *Shakuntala* all the plays were inspired by Prithviji, partly dictated, sometimes written and mostly added to in the form of extempore dialogue by Prithviji. They were truly his creations, a product of his imagination, voicing his lament for injustice and the ills of his motherland, and showing ways of rising above it all to a glorious future. The themes of the plays were uncomplicated, the language predominantly Hindustani, a simplified combination of Hindi and Urdu understood all over north India, and their style was naturalistic, with melodrama overtaking some of the climaxes.

'The plays created an unprecedented sensation wherever we went. Carrying along our own cooks and utensils, we stayed in rented houses, younger children and their ayahs travelling with mothers. During the holidays even school kids joined the cavalcade. One tour followed another and as the years progressed, we collected humanity to this nucleus like a massive avalanche…poets, writers, convicts or mere observers, all were welcome.'

According to an editorial in *Natya*, 'The theatre which Prithviraj established was not an ordinary professional company. It was a vehicle for the expression of dedicated idealism. This also required courage. The ideals that he tried to portray: national unity, racial amity, domestic concord, were all crumbling under the onslaught of reactionary forces which were bent upon

cleaving the country apart. But such was the passion of his plays, so supercharged with sincerity, that they were a wonder to behold…There was never anything nearly (sic) like it in Indian drama…The impact of Prithvi Theatres was remarkable. It showed the magnetic power of ideas and the strength of theatre which deals with contemporaneous problems. Thousands were drawn to this dynamic drama. The influence of the company on the course of events was of little value, however. Rarely is it given to the artist or to theatre to alter history.'

However, in 1944, Prithviraj foresaw communal problems in India and commissioned Inderraj Anand and Ramesh Saigal to write *Deewar*, an allegorical story of two brothers Suresh and Ramesh separated by a foreign woman. He couldn't have known then, that along with India's independence from British rule, would come the Partition and the creation of Pakistan. The play was also eerily prescient in that it

Above left: Zohra Segal, Prithviraj Kapoor and Sajjan in *Deewar*.

Facing page: Prithviraj Kapoor with Sajjan in *Deewar*.

Left: Zohra Segal as the 'Foreign Woman' in *Deewar*, who creates a rift between two brothers. Zohra, Uzra Mumtaz's sister, joined Prithvi Theatres as a dance director and went on to act in several productions.

Above right: Uzra Mumtaz in *Deewar*.

Inset: Sajjan was associated with Prithvi Theatres for many years and went on to act in several films as a hero, villain and character actor.

ended with the wall separating the homes of the two brothers being broken down—just as today India and Pakistan strive to mend fences after years of animosity.

Geoffrey Kendal who saw a performance of *Deewar* at the Royal Opera House, wrote in *Shakespearewallah*, 'It is the story of two brothers, and can also be the story of two different systems. This is the story of the woman who drew the line of blood between the brothers. This can also be the story of that third party who in the last 150 years of its reign has added many bloody chapters to our pages of history, who has left now but

whose footprints are still deeply engraved and are burning like sparks of fire on our hard-earned freedom. In other words, it was all about British rule and the evils of Partition. The play began with a scene of singing and thanksgiving, while the two brothers Suresh, played by Prithviraj and Ramesh, played by Sajjan, were beaming and embracing each other. Then, one stormy night, a foreign woman and her companions come to the door for shelter. Soon Suresh and Ramesh had taken off their dhotis and turbans and appeared in check shirts, riding breeches, and boots. Finally, the female John Bull figure suggests that the two of them live separately. So Ramesh demands partition, and a wall of large bricks is set up, right down the middle of the stage.

'The brothers are separated. The woman was the one who had the greatest hand in all this. The wall of hatred was the only support she had. Ramesh (Pakistan) was obstinate; Suresh (India) was hopeless. Then came a storm and the people cried, "We do not want the wall!" At this point the peasants swarmed in with picks and crowbars and knocked the bricks all over the stage. Ramesh and Suresh embraced again, and the company chanted the lines, "We were One. We are One. We will remain One." There was much singing and dancing, lengthy heart-to-hearts between the characters, and some excellent acting, particularly from one of Prithviraj's sons (Raj Kapoor), as one of the servants. The production, with its huge cast, was polished and effective. We met Prithviraj during one of the intervals—the show was four-and-a half-hours long. At the end he made a long speech in Hindi (adding bits in English for our benefit), mainly to say that, after all, it was not really the foreigners' fault! As we left the theatre he was standing in the foyer; a great figure like a Roman Elder, bowing and holding a begging-bowl, not for his theatre, but for a charity.'

Deewar opened on 9 August 1945. The British censors objected to the anti-Imperialist message in the play. There are two versions of how Prithviraj actually managed to get the clearance certificate. According to one version, he went to meet the official who had stamped his objection on the pages. Prithviraj was a charismatic star and it was easy for him to charm the man into giving him the file so that he could personally speak to a higher official. On his way to the other office, he tore out the offending page, got the higher man's okay and staged the play. According to the other version, Prithviraj argued his case for artistic expression passionately before the British official and forced him to okay the script. He later told his group, 'My law studies were finally of some use.'

Zohra Segal, who played the part of the foreign woman, had to smoke a cigarette in the role. She would take a few puffs and head for the wings where a young Raj Kapoor, who was playing the role of the servant, would be waiting impatiently to grab the burning cigarette from her. Later when Shammi took over the same role, he too would wait in the wings for the cigarette. Shashi was the only one of the brothers who never took to smoking.

In the early production of *Deewar*, little Shashi used to play a small role as the main protagonist's son. 'In the first act of *Deewar*, this child sees some foreigners have arrived,' Shashi recalls. 'Among them is a lady. Pointing to the foreigner, the child says, *"Main usse shaadi karoonga."* (I shall marry her.) I used to say that even when I was 7—and I carried on saying that line until I was 10 or 12. Little did I know that I actually would marry a foreigner. My father was interested in astrology and he had predicted when I was in my late teens that I would get involved with somebody *"saat samunder paar"*!' (from across the seven seas).

In *I Go South*, Professor Dayal writes, 'Prithvi played *Deewar* fearlessly through thick and thin and recognition of the play as a powerful force came at long last from high-up leaders. Sardar Patel sat through the play, though he had come merely to put in

Above: A still from *Pathan* with Prithviraj Kapoor playing the role of Sher Khan. Fourth from left is Raj Kapoor, playing his son Bahadur Khan.

Above left: Kuldeep Kaur playing the role of Bahadur Khan's wife in *Deewar*. Kaur was film star and politician Govinda's paternal aunt. In 1958 Jennifer Kapoor played this role and uttered only one word *'Kahan?'*

Right: Prithviraj Kapoor and Shammi Kapoor after a show of *Pathan*.

Facing page above: Prithviraj Kapoor making a speech for communal harmony after a show of *Deewar*.

Below: Sardar Vallabhbhai Patel (extreme right) watching a show of *Deewar*.

an official appearance. *Deewar* drew from him laughter and tears, and after the fall of the final curtain, a half-hour speech, the repercussion of which was exemption for Prithvi Theatres from the entertainment tax.'

MUMBAI HAD A PUNJAB FRONTIER Association and Prithviraj Kapoor was the President. At one of the meetings some Pathans told him that people in India who were not familiar with Frontier culture, made fun of them, calling them *darban* (gatekeeper) or *soodkhor* (loan shark) Pathans.

Prithviraj, who always considered himself a Pathan first and foremost, decided to do something to do away with these erroneous stereotypes and also further the cause of Hindu-Muslim unity. At his behest, his friend Lal Chand Bismil from Peshawar wrote *Pathan*, considered to be Prithvi Theatres' finest play.

Pathan opened on 13 April 1947. It had the most realistic sets and costumes, which

(village) of Peshawar, where dawn was slowly breaking. And we watched entranced, we lost ourselves in the play, captivated till the end of the show when we returned to our world.'

In the play, a Hindu Diwan sacrifices his life to save his master, Sher Khan, a Muslim Pathan, during a surprise enemy attack. Years after this incident, on the wedding night of the Pathan's son, the Diwan's son kills a bandit in self-defence when accompanying his wife to her parents' home. In the battle that ensues between the two clans several men are killed. The Muslims agree to a truce only if the Hindu murderer is handed over to

them. To save the life of the Diwan's son, Sher Khan offers himself. But only the sacrifice of a young man can appease the enemy clan's wrath. So Sher Khan hands over his only son Bahadur Khan, who had been born after many years of prayer. Bahadur Khan's bride lets out a scream at which Sher Khan chides her for cowardice. Zohra Segal writes in *Stages*, 'The impact of this sacrifice was soul-stirring and there was not a dry eye in the house whenever we reached the end of the third act. The noble ideals of the play pierced the hearts of the spectators and brought whatever was best in

Raj Kapoor had handpicked himself in Peshawar. He had recently got married, and took his wife Krishna with him on the shopping trip to buy jackets, turbans, kurtas, shalwars and Pathan shoes with thick soles made out of tyres.

Shaukat Kaifi says, 'When the curtains went up, the atmosphere of the play created a kind of magic which enveloped the performers in such a way that they believed they were actually part of the milieu. It seemed as if we had reached some *garhi*

Left and middle: Prithviraj Kapoor being felicitated after a show of *Pathan*.

Right: Prithviraj Kapoor standing outside the auditorium with his famous *'jholi'*, collecting donations for various social causes. Premnath is on the right.

their nature to the surface. Apart from its overpowering dramatic content this production was the most artistic in the entire repertoire.

'Prithviji as Sher Khan, lord and master of the fortress, was every inch a Pathan in his speech and bearing, bringing all his inherent magnanimity, earthiness and ruggedness to the character. What is more, he looked a devout Muslim, so much so that when Uzra's mother-in-law came to see the play, she refused to believe that he was a Hindu.

"There is an inner spirituality shining through the man which only a Muslim could be blessed with," she declared!'

Years later, Shashi Kapoor played Bahadur Khan (the role was originally played by Raj Kapoor). Says Shashi, 'In the third act Bahadur Khan gets married and when I performed in the play, I had just got married. I had had a very simple marriage. Jennifer and I had flown in from Singapore to get married in front of my parents because I had promised my mother I would. Shammiji had married without her knowledge, and that had caused her a lot of unhappiness.'

When Shashi was to get married, Prithviraj was shooting the climax of *Mughal-e-Azam* in Jaipur. K. Asif organized a special plane for Papaji to come to Bombay just for the evening to attend the wedding of his youngest son, and return to Jaipur immediately after it was over. There was no night landing facility at Jaipur at that time, so Prithviraj had to wait till the plane could land at dawn, and then went straight to the sets.

Shashi remembers going to Pune to act in *Pathan* soon after this. 'As the father of the bridegroom, Papaji looked at me and spat. Pathans do this to ward off the evil eye. My bride, who was playing the bride in the play as well, was appalled. "Why did he spit at you?" she asked. I told her it was a very auspicious thing to do. After that, she did the same thing with our children, not really spit, but just *thoo thoo*.'

While Shashi's parents welcomed the new bride, Geoffrey Kendal was not too pleased with the marriage. He felt he was

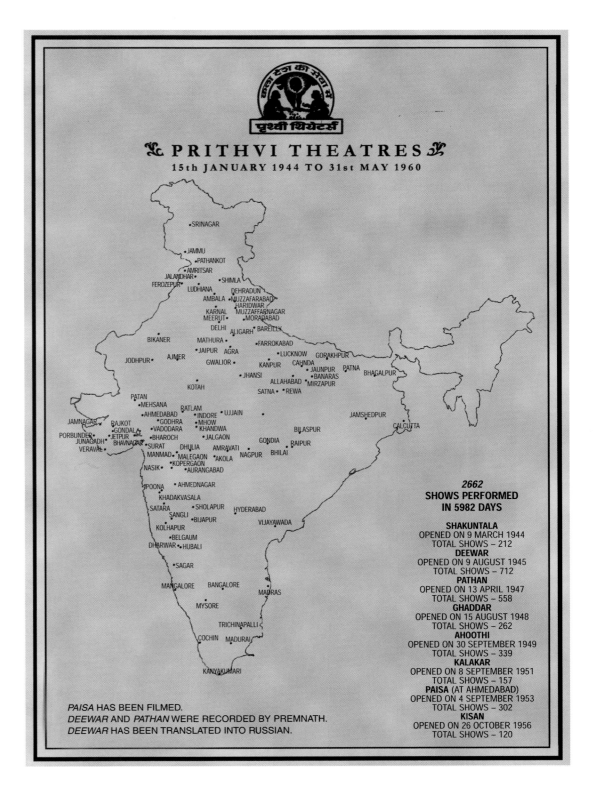

PRITHVI THEATRES
15th JANUARY 1944 TO 31st MAY 1960

2662
**SHOWS PERFORMED
IN 5982 DAYS**

SHAKUNTALA
OPENED ON 9 MARCH 1944
TOTAL SHOWS – 212
DEEWAR
OPENED ON 9 AUGUST 1945
TOTAL SHOWS – 712
PATHAN
OPENED ON 13 APRIL 1947
TOTAL SHOWS – 558
GHADDAR
OPENED ON 15 AUGUST 1948
TOTAL SHOWS – 262
AHOOTHI
OPENED ON 30 SEPTEMBER 1949
TOTAL SHOWS – 339
KALAKAR
OPENED ON 8 SEPTEMBER 1951
TOTAL SHOWS – 157
PAISA (AT AHMEDABAD)
OPENED ON 4 SEPTEMBER 1953
TOTAL SHOWS – 302
KISAN
OPENED ON 26 OCTOBER 1956
TOTAL SHOWS – 120

PAISA HAS BEEN FILMED.
DEEWAR AND *PATHAN* WERE RECORDED BY PREMNATH.
DEEWAR HAS BEEN TRANSLATED INTO RUSSIAN.

losing not just his daughter, but his Viola, Desdemona and Ophelia. And the set, props and costumes coordinator. His displeasure lasted till his grandson Kunal was born. One look at the child and all was forgiven and forgotten.

'I also remember,' says Shashi, 'doing *Pathan* in winter in the north. In *Pathan* and *Deewar* certain characters were supposed to have blonde hair because they were foreigners. They had to colour their hair for the show, then wash it out afterwards. Since there was no water in the theatre, they had to come back to our lodgings and bathe in freezing cold water.'

When *Pathan* was staged in Bombay, some Pathans from Bhendi Bazar had heard rumours that the play made derogatory references to them. So they landed up at the Royal Opera House during one of the

Above: Sudarshan Sethi, Shriram Shastri and Prithviraj Kapoor in *Ghaddar*.

Left: Uzra Mumtaz and Prithviraj Kapoor in *Ghaddar*.

Right: Zohra Segal playing the faithful servant in *Ghaddar*.

Facing page: Kashinath Bhatt and Prithviraj Kapoor in *Ahoothi*.

performances, with the intention of disrupting the show. But after seeing the entire play, they were so moved that they went up on stage and danced.

Prithviraj's brother-in-law Vishwa Mehra, known by everyone as Mamaji, recalls Hindu-Muslim riots breaking out in Delhi before *Pathan* was to be staged there. The tour was diverted to Jodhpur, where the troupe stayed in comfort at the palace. The Maharaja came to see one of the shows. During the performance, the Maharaja's staff came in with drinks for him. Prithviraj asked for the drinks to be removed, and the Maharaja bowed to his wishes. He waited until the interval to go out of the hall and have a drink. Prithviraj also refused expensive gifts from the Maharaja and just requested him to pay the rent of the stadium where the troupe was performing.

Prithviraj did not drink himself. At times when he was unwell and was advised to drink brandy, he would take some in a bowl, pray and gulp it down. Mamaji says he did not smoke either till almost the age of 40, but once he started, he smoked just about everything in sight—cigarettes, bidis, cheroots . . .

THE INDIVIDUAL AND COLLECTIVE horrors of Partition left Prithviraj totally grief-stricken. 'Now I will have to get a visa to go to my own homeland,' he lamented. Many of his Muslim friends—Noorjehan, Manto, Beena, Swarnlata and Nazir among them—left for Pakistan. With his limited means, he did everything he could to provide relief in cash and kind to the stream of refugees coming into India, who appealed to him for help.

His anguish took the form of a play, *Ghaddar*, written by Inderraj Anand. The play, which opened on 15 August 1948, told the story of the patriotic Muslims who stayed back in India after Partition and were branded as traitors.

In *Ghaddar*, a Muslim nationalist leader in India, Mohammad Ashraf, goes to prison

for his anti-British activities. His wife is left to fend for herself. Her 'friends' talk her into persuading her husband to join the Muslim League. He is shocked by Partition and shattered by the communal bloodshed that follows in its wake His wife takes it for granted that they will migrate to Pakistan, but after a bloody encounter with rioters, Ashraf decides to stay back in India to try and undo the harm done by his partymen. In the end he is shot down by his own partymen who see him as a traitor.

Shaukat Kaifi recollects that in *Ghaddar*, Papaji had called Mohammad Ali Jinnah a traitor because he had put forth the demand for a separate Muslim state, Pakistan. 'When we were touring the south, in Cochin some Muslim League people protested against *Ghaddar*. They threatened to burn down the theatre if this play was performed.'

When the play opened, tensions grew and each member of the cast felt a sense of unease and fear. Dealing with people who had made the play an emotional and communal issue clearly required the utmost sensitivity, for even a casual remark could spark off a full-scale conflagration in which lives could be lost. Prithviraj decided to exercise all the charm and tact he possessed to defuse the tension. He invited some of the protestors to come and watch the play. After that, if they still felt that it was

offensive, they were free to do as
they pleased.

The protesters accepted his invitation. At
the end of the show, they came up on stage,
hugged Prithviraj warmly, congratulated him
and left as friends. The entire cast breathed a
sigh of relief. Prithviraj's natural Pathan
warmth and camaraderie had won the day
once again.

Prayag Raj recounts a similar incident in
Mumbai. Prithviraj sent the Muslim League
protesters a letter promising to discontinue
the play if they found anything objectionable
about it. And the protestors did turn up. After
the show, Prithviraj went and stood outside
the Royal Opera House where the play was
being staged. Prayag Raj remembers peering

down from the terrace of the Royal Opera
House—a sea of white kurta pyjama-clad
Muslims were jostling each other and
straining to shake Prithviraj's hand.

He has another *Ghaddar* story to tell as
well. 'We were rehearsing for the play just
before the rains in Indore,' he recalls. 'A brand
new set had been erected in an outdoor
pandal (marquee). Suddenly a violent storm
broke out. The central pillar cracked and the
whole *pandal* came crashing down on the set
and on the actors. Prithviraj covered two or
three actors with his own body and took the
impact of the crashing pillar on himself. I
remember this as vividly as a scene straight
out of a film. The set was ruined and the
show had to be postponed for a week. We

were all thoroughly shaken up by the
incident, but Prithviraj remained calm and
unperturbed. He sent for *jalebis* for everyone
to celebrate the fact that no one was hurt.'

Clearly, Prithviraj Kapoor had the knack
of weathering storms, ideological or
otherwise, with great aplomb.

Once, on tour, one of the workers called
Dhondu suddenly came down with cholera.
Nobody dared to go near him and the
stench from the room where the ailing
worker lay, was nauseating. When Prithviraj,
who had gone out for a few hours, returned
and learnt about Dhondu's illness, he went
straight up to him and hugged him. He was
neither put off by the vomit all over the
room, nor was he afraid of contracting the

Left: Pushpa and Ravindra Kapoor in *Paisa*. Pushpa married fellow actor Prayag Raj.

Above: Premnath in *Ghaddar*. He was Prithviraj Kapoor's cousin (maternal uncle's son), who also became a famous film star. Premnath's brothers Narendranath and Rajendranath were also film actors.

Facing page left: Shammi Kapoor and Uzra Mumtaz in *Kalakar*.

Facing page right: Uzra Mumtaz and Prithviraj Kapoor in *Paisa*.

disease himself. He just stayed by Dhondu's side, comforting and reassuring him till the doctor arrived. Prithviraj's impromptu act of kindness and insistence that medical aid arrived without delay, saved Dhondu's life.

Dhondu's son Sharad was educated by Jennifer Kapoor, and now works with Shashi Kapoor's elder son Kunal.

Shaukat Kaifi remembers another occasion when the troupe was travelling by bus in Kashmir, and a roadside labourer fell down and hurt himself. Prithviraj, who saw this happen, immediately asked the driver to turn the bus around and drive back to where the injured man lay groaning and writhing in

Above left: Young Shashi Kapoor as the villain Gayadin in *Kisan*.

Above right: Kiran Segal, Pushpa, Prithviraj Kapoor, Uzra Mumtaz in *Kisan*. Kiran is Zohra Segal's daughter and an Odissi dancer.

pain. He got the troupe's doctor to administer him first aid, took him to a local hospital and gave him some money for his treatment. Only then did the troupe resume its journey.

The plight of refugees after Partition formed the central theme of Prithvi Theatres' fifth play *Ahoothi* (Sacrifice), again written by Lal Chand Bismil. The play, which opened on 30 September 1949, dealt with the fate of a Hindu girl abducted during the post-Partition riots. Though she is accepted back by her family and fiancé, her future in-laws and the rest of society condemn her as 'polluted'. Eventually, to save her family's honour, she commits suicide.

When *Ahoothi* was being written, Prithviraj and others in the troupe felt it was time he took a break from always playing the lead, and so the central role in the play was that of the abducted girl's mother. Uzra Mumtaz was to play the role but panicked and felt she would not be able to carry it off. So the play had to be rewritten with Prithviraj back in the saddle as the main protagonist, but since a sturdy man could not possibly speak the lines meant for a helpless woman, the character was turned into an old, blind man. The role of the hapless girl was played by Pushpa.

The next play by Prithvi Theatres, *Kalakar*, changed the fortunes of Shammi Kapoor. He had already started acting in films since 1952-53 and had done some good roles like *Rail Ka Dibba* and *Laila Majnu*, but his career had yet to take off. His elder brother Raj Kapoor, was by then a well-established star and filmmaker, who had actually directed his father in *Awara*. The film had four generations of Kapoors acting in it—Raj Kapoor's grandfather Bashesharnath, his father Prithviraj, himself, younger brother Shashi, and a very small Randhir, Raj Kapoor's son, who appeared during the credits. To this day, it is a record unmatched in the history of cinema anywhere in the world.

In the third act of *Kalakar* Shammi Kapoor appeared as a rich, modern, playboy—a role that led to his 'big break'. After seeing Shammi in *Kalakar*, producer S. Mukherjee of Filmistan Studio, director Nasir Hussain and music composer O.P. Nayyar were thoroughly impressed, and signed him on for *Tumsa Nahin Dekha*.

This Shammi-starrer turned out to be a trendsetter. He acquired the image of a rebel, and went on to become a big star, and one of the best dancers in showbiz. Even today, Shammi Kapoor's songs make popular remixes, and his style of dancing is copied by young stars.

Written by Ramanand Sagar, *Kalakar* opened on 8 September 1951. In *Kalakar* an artist falls in love with a tribal girl Gaura. Instead of abandoning her as he did in the original version (Prithviraj rewrote the entire third act himself, because he felt that it portrayed artists in a negative light), the artist marries her and takes her to the city, where she is corrupted by her newfound wealth and freedom, and is attracted to a rich young man who tries to seduce her. But after a few rude shocks, Gaura learns her lesson and returns, contrite, to her husband.

Zohra Segal had composed a brilliant masked dance for *Kalakar*, which Shashi Kapoor remembers performing soon after his marriage to Jennifer. With her fair skin and high cheekbones, Jennifer passed off as a mountain girl and also did some tribal dances in the play.

In Prithvi Theatres' post-Independence plays, Prithviraj gradually moved on from portraying national problems to examining social issues.

Prithvi Theatres' sixth production, *Paisa*, opened on 4 September 1953. *Paisa*, as the title indicates, was about greed and how it transformed a simple and honest bank manager into an avaricious monster. After losing his family and friends, and causing

misery to all around him, he reforms in the end.

The post-Independence years also saw a change in the fortunes of theatre, not for the better. The audience for plays was fast dwindling, thanks to the growing allure of the silver screen, and the Gondals, who owned the Royal Opera House had restricted theatre performances to morning shows only. The constant shortage of funds tempted Papaji to turn *Paisa* into a film. Though he had a roster of top stars willing to work for him, he insisted on casting his theatre team in the film.

When the film was half way through, the financier decided to pull out. Prithviraj immediately dipped into his earnings from films to complete *Paisa*. The film, unfortunately, bombed at the box-office. Even for Prithviraj, who was used to weathering storms, this was quite a big blow. The financier even tried to stop him and the troupe from leaving the city till his dues were cleared. Eventually Raj Kapoor bailed him out of the situation. Not one to be indebted to anyone, even a son, Papaji repaid him later. He cleared the last bit of debt from the money he made from films.

Despite the financial imbroglio *Paisa* had got Prithviraj into, he remained unfazed by the film's failure. He told the troupe there was no reason to lose heart. 'God has taught me a lesson,' he said. 'Why did a stage lover venture into films? He wants us to carry on in the service of Hindi theatre.'

IN 1955, DR RAJENDRA PRASAD THE President of India at that time, asked

Above: Chinese Premier Chou En-lai with Balraj Sahni and Prithviraj Kapoor who were part of a cultural delegation to China in 1956.

Left: The Prithvi Theatres team in 1958. Seated extreme left is Jennifer newly married to Shashi Kapoor, standing in the back row third from the right. Seated fifth from left is Prithviraj Kapoor's first heroine *'Cinema Girl'* Ermeline, who later became an actress in the theatre.

Prithviraj Kapoor to do a play on farmers. So Prithvi Theatres' eighth production *Kisan* premiered on 26 October 1956.

'I was all of 18 and the production designer. I did the lighting, costumes and sound,' recalls Shashi Kapoor. 'Uzraji and Shaukatji were very helpful with the costumes. Shaukatji was helpful with the music also—it was Uttar Pradesh folk.

'*Kisan* was set in a village. It was about

the farmers' reaction to automation technology being ushered in. They called a tractor *lohe ka haathi* (iron elephant). *Kisan* was a debate on the pros and cons of the issue woven into an emotional story about the Chaudhary and his children. His wife goes mad during a famine. *Lagaan* (2001) had some bits from *Kisan*.

'I was proud of the fact that I was able to create the impression of rain … we used to get a thundering applause for the effects.

'I had a small part—of the baddie— in this play. It was in 1958 that I started playing juvenile leads, the grown-up leads being played by Rajji, Shammiji, Premnathji. I was

also the henchman of the rich zamindars and moneylenders who exploited the farmers. I remember, in the beginning of the last act of *Kisan*, I had to laugh a vicious laugh, while walking from one end of the stage to the other, and I just couldn't do it in one breath. It was particularly tough in the Royal Opera House where the width of the stage is about 40 feet. I could never get it right.'

WHEN SHASHI KAPOOR BECAME THE assistant stage manager of Prithvi Theatres, he tried to bring in new techniques of lighting, though very little material was available locally. That meant innumerable

trips to Chor Bazaar— Mumbai's famous flea market—where almost anything could be acquired secondhand. 'Prithvi Theatres had a very conservative system of lighting,' he recalls. 'It was all within the proscenium—from the footlights onwards going upstage—but never out of the proscenium. By the mid '50s, I had had the opportunity to see productions that came from abroad, like the MRA (Moral ReArmament) Company that staged shows at the Excelsior Theatre. I realized you could light from much beyond the proscenium as well. I would have fights with the lighting people who wouldn't let me do things my way.'

'Shri Prithviraj Kapoor has been a pioneer in the resurrection of our professional theatre. His personality, his genuine love of the theatre and his deep interest in the problems facing society have combined to earn him a special place in the world of modern Indian theatre. His plays truly mirror the complexities of our times and yet are excellent entertainment.

I send my good wishes.'

INDIRA GANDHI

'Once, the fellow who was in charge of lighting tied a heavy K2 studio light on the balcony at Bhartiya Vidya Bhavan. When I asked him, "What if it falls on people's heads?", he just laughed at me. Well, during a show of *Pathan*, the light actually did fall. Luckily this happened during the interval when people had gone out for a short while. We just had enough time to rush out and camouflage everything.'

BY THIS TIME (1959-60), PRITHVIRAJ HAD started losing his voice. Over sixteen years of acting on stage, making public speeches and talking almost non-stop to the troupe, he had put his voice under tremendous strain. He hated mikes and never used one. In the Royal Opera House, fans were switched off when a performance was on, and spectators were given hand fans which they often took home as souvenirs! By the end of the '50s, Prithviraj's vocal chords had taken such a beating that in one of his last films *Teen Bahuraniyan*, his voice had to be dubbed by another actor.

Many members of Prithvi Theatres started leaving to work in films. Prithviraj did not stop anyone, not even his own sons. B.M. Vyas says, 'He told me, "You are flying high, give me a lift." '

He was sent abroad on many cultural delegations by the then Prime Minister of India, Pandit Jawaharlal Nehru; he was a fellow of the Sangeet Natak Akademi, but he refused any government aid for Prithvi Theatres. He felt that taking money meant for theatre and putting it into his own theatre, would be like taking money from one pocket and putting it into another.

Once, when Prithviraj had to decline a cultural tour because a play had not had its full run, Panditji chided him for not having an understudy for his roles. Zohra Segal records an interesting exchange between the two in *Stages*. 'I know someone else who is without an understudy,' said Prithviraj. 'Who?' asked Panditji. 'You!' replied the actor.'

By 1960, Prithvi Theatres had journeyed across the length and breadth of India for 16 years, taking Hindi theatre to the common man's doorstep. Founded by a man who believed that theatre was worship, and who would lose his voice while perfecting his art, Prithvi Theatres finally closed down in May 1960—because there could never be an understudy for that man.

Nora Richards with an unidentified woman in Andretta, her retirement home.

My dear dear dear Noraji,

Thank you ever so much for your affectionate letter, so full of love-like your very self. Yes—it is true—I had to cry halt and declare. 'The party is over.'

I consider myself very fortunate that God gave me sixteen long years of theatre life with full freedom to say what I wanted to say and do what I wanted to do on the stage.

The audiences bore with me till the final curtain and so did my colleagues. Only my poor throat could not bear my rough treatment any further and gave up the ghost. Poor thing had been groaning under the load of the heavy roles I had burdened it with from the very start but bore on patiently till 1957 when the cracks started looking rather visible and the groans more audible so much so that the doctors started advising I must give it a day off every third day, which you know is not possible for any theatre man who had to pay twenty thousand as salaries every month Still I plodded on and on—thunder, rain or storm till I reached a spot where my throat could not and would not budge an inch further. A poet has said:

Bahut shauq se sun raha tha zamana
Hameen so gaye dastan kehte kehte

See what has happened here—my blue pen gave up the ghost—had exhausted its ink—just like the theatre man in Prithvi—I have kept up writing with the red pen—so will I keep up—my work—through the film Prithvi—till the Theatre Prithvi is refilled—revived—but he would be able to write on this page with the blue pen—I do not know—I do not know.

So whether the Theatre Prithvi would be able to give any more plays in this life—I do not know—I do not know—the page is running out fast—the blue pen is lying there inkless and exhausted—like our Theatre Prithvi. It is past midnight. I shall wait for the dawn—and with the new sun I shall write again with the blue pen. Good night then.

Lo and behold the night is over and there is the dawn the new day—the new sun is rising and with that I get back my blue pen fully charged with the blue ink, and I turn a new page.

Who knows there may be like that a new dawn in Prithvi's life and the Theatre Prithvi—fully recharged and equipped may be able to turn a new page and write on that in bold letter once again:

THE THEATRE

I have been a bloody optimist all my life and have always sung aloud with the poet: 'If hopes are dupes—fears may be liars.' With God's grace and yours and Lalaji's blessings my voice is regaining strength and I hope and pray it would not be long before it is strong enough to shoulder the brunt of film Prithvi and then one day the Theatre Prithvi as well. Amen.

There were hardly eleven shows performed from the 1st of January till the 10th of April—but thank God with the help of Raj and Shammi, I could pay 5 months salaries i.e. till the 31st May the closing day. Some of the boys and girls have been absorbed in the films here—some are still struggling for a foothold. It's a pity. I pray for them day and night that they all may get settled properly and on better jobs.

With love and respects.

Prithvi
Council Hall, Poona
14th September 1948

Scene IV: The Dream

OVER 16 YEARS, PRITHVI Theatres gave a total of 2,662 performances over 5982 days in 112 places, with Prithviraj Kapoor appearing in every single show—a play every alternate day. It would have been an impossible feat for a lesser man than him.

Shashi Kapoor says, 'People thought a film star was doing it as a hobby or for a lark, but Papaji didn't believe in amateur theatre.'

He needed to work in films to keep Prithvi Theatres alive, or else he would have given all his time to theatre. Once when Prithvi Theatres was touring the north, K. Asif came to request Prithviraj for extra dates for *Mughal-e-Azam*. Even though the salaries of

Prithvi Theatres were being paid out of the money that he was earning from the film, Prithviraj did not abandon the tour.

Sometime in 1949 when Uzra Mumtaz went to visit Prithviraj on the sets of V. Shantaram's *Dahej*, she remarked: 'What a

difference watching him on stage and then on the sets. I told him it was like having seen a lion in the jungle and then watching him perform tricks in the circus. Prithviraj had a good laugh over it and said, "I really feel that way. When I go on the sets, I put my tail between my legs and I jump into the cage." '

AT THE TIME THAT PRITHVI THEATRES WAS touring the country with its repertoire of Hindi plays, Geoffrey Kendal's Shakespeareana was visiting the same cities and towns with plays in English.

Kendal writes in *Shakespearewallah*, 'We met Prithviraj many times all over the place, and eventually his youngest son, Shashi, became our son-in-law. Prithvi signed his letters to us, "Yours fraternally", and I think that is what he felt. If his company was in

Bombay and we were going on tour, Prithvi and his wife would meet us at Dadar Station. They were usually a little late, but we would see this great white-clad figure striding over the railway bridge followed by his tiny wife. A bearer would come behind with a great basket of food for our actors: tandoori chicken, naans, and perhaps mangoes if they were in season. There was always a shine in his eye and a cheerful smile as he waved us on our way. It was a benediction from one who knew that a benediction was needed.'

The young Shashi Kapoor was fated to meet Jennifer Kendal under oddly 'theatrical' circumstances. It happened in 1956 in Calcutta. Prithvi Theatres was having a very successful season at the Empire Theatre—which eventually became a cinema hall. Some former Prithvi Theatres troupers, and stars like Raj and Shammi Kapoor and Premnath had come down for a few days to boost ticket sales. As the shows were running to packed houses, the Empire Theatre management extended the season, as a result of which Shakespeareana had to wait their turn to perform at the theatre. They would spend their days performing in school and college halls and some of the members would turn up to see the Prithvi Theatres' performance at the Empire in the evening.

'We were staying in a place called Ritz Continental Hotel,' recalls Shashi. 'I was 18 then, the assistant stage manager and also doing small roles. It was the prerogative of the ASM to peep through the curtain to look at the audience before each show and see if everything was okay. But one day when I did that, I saw a very beautiful face, which I first

Above: Laura and Geoffrey Kendal in *Dear Liar* at Prithvi Theatre in 1984.

Facing page: Jennifer shares a moment with her husband Shashi Kapoor.

thought looked Russian. There had been an invasion of Russians tourists at RK Studio because of the success of *Awara* in Russia. Since part of the time I was attending shoots as an apprentice at RK Studio, I would often meet these Russians—fair, red, good-looking, they used to be.

'I liked what I saw. I told my friend Tiger to find out who she was. He said that she and some others were guests of the owners of the Empire Theatre. The next day, she was there again and in the same seat, with a group of people. For the next three to four days, they were there for four different

Geoffrey Kendal as Malvolio in *Twelfth Night*.

performances. It was my cousin Subbiraj who finally found out who she was. They were staying in Sudder Street at Hotel Fairlawn behind Empire. Subbiraj offered to introduce us though he didn't know her.

'At Fairlawn, the reception area leads to an open dining room. When we arrived at the hotel, they were having their dinner there. Subbiraj introduced himself and us. She looked up and went back to her soup. And I was gaga. I didn't make an impression but she did.

'I discovered that this was the company waiting for Prithvi Theatres to get out of Empire Theatre because we had extended our season. I saw a couple of their performances at school and college matinees. That's where I came to know them but not much. She didn't really look at me.

'After a few months we came back to Bombay. One day I was doing the lighting at the Royal Opera House for our new production *Kisan*. It was early in the morning. One of the carpenters came rushing to me and said a *mem* had come to meet me. I dropped everything immediately and rushed out. And there she was sitting on the steps with her dog. I almost stopped breathing.

'She said, "We are here in Bombay and we should meet." She was staying very near the Royal Opera House—at Grant Road in a place called Church Mission House, which still exists. Usually I used to get off the local train at Charni Road, but I started getting off at Grant Road, which was a longer walk. From the station I would go to Church Mission House to meet her and then go on to the Royal Opera House. Likewise, she

A young Jennifer Kendal as Viola in Shakespeareana's *Twelfth Night*.

would come and see me. Near the Royal Opera House, is a small dhaba called Mathura Dairy Farm. In 1956, *puri bhaji* cost 4 annas—we used to eat there quite often. I had had no girlfriend till then, which was rather unusual for a Kapoor. I was shy and too involved with my work.

'She told me later that initially she felt I might be gay because I didn't respond much to her. And you know that in India, whenever buddies are hanging around together, we often hold hands—a gesture of male bonding quite acceptable here, but in the West they find it odd.

'Coming from a typical English theatrical company full of gays, it wasn't so far-fetched for her to wonder if I was gay too. A few months down the line, however, she realized that I wasn't.'

In 1956, when Geoffrey Kendal happened to run short of actors, he wrote to Prithviraj

Above: Shashi Kapoor as Cassio, Geoffrey Kendal as Othello, Brian Kellet as Iago and Frank Wheatly as Montano in *Othello*. This was Shashi Kapoor's first role with Shakespeareana in 1956.

Left: Jennifer Kendal as Ophelia in *Hamlet*.

Facing page: The Shakespeareana Troupe in 1955. *Back row:* Utpal Dutt, Connor Farrington, Geoffrey Kendal, Anwar Mirza, John Day. *Front row:* Frank Wheatly, Nancy Neal, Felicity Kendal, Laura Liddel (Kendal), Jennifer Kendal, Wendy Beavis and Brian Kellet. Utpal Dutt became a leading light on Kolkata's theatre scene and also acted in films.

asking him if he could lend him Shashi for a while. One of Geoffrey's juvenile leads was leaving for England and he needed a young actor to replace him. So, in February 1957, Shashi Kapoor joined Shakespeareana in Bangalore.

His future father-in-law was a tough

'I was with Shakespeareana till the middle of 1958,' says Shashi. 'Then I rejoined Prithvi Theatres with Jennifer, who did small roles without much dialogue, and helped with other things like props. Then we kept shuttling between the two companies. When Shakespeareana came to India, Jennifer

'Papaji didn't want to keep the theatre going,' says Shashi Kapoor. 'Eventually he closed down the theatre primarily because of his failing health, and also because he felt that the best acting talent used theatre as a stepping stone to films.'

Prithviraj Kapoor's voice had started

taskmaster. Within three weeks, Shashi had to learn 14 speaking parts, including six juvenile leads. He played Lysander in *A Midsummer Night's Dream*, Cassio in *Othello*, Bassanio in *Merchant of Venice*, Banquo in *Macbeth*. Kendal was sparing in his praise—putting a bottle of Bulmer's Woodpecker cider in the changing room was his way of showing appreciation.

would be with them and I would be with Prithvi Theatres.'

IN 1947 RAJ KAPOOR STARTED HIS OWN film company—RK Studio. Shammi Kapoor started acting in films about five years later, and by 1957 both brothers had become big stars. There was no question of either of them returning to theatre.

failing in the late '50s. Some of his diary entries around this time are quite revealing. He wrote of instances when he carried on acting despite acute pain in his throat. He wrote heartrending pleas to God to save his voice. Prayag Raj recalls a rare instance when Prithviraj actually wanted to cancel a show because his voice had completely packed up. The audience, however, refused to take a

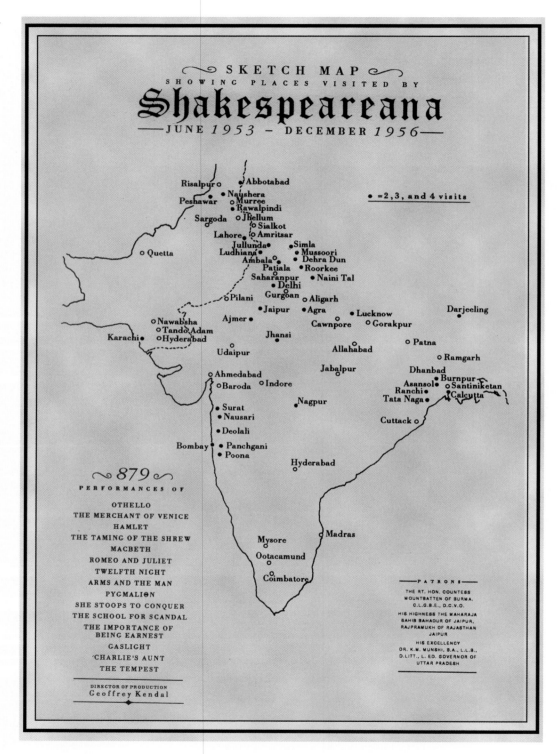

SKETCH MAP

SHOWING PLACES VISITED BY

Shakespeareana

—JUNE 1953 – DECEMBER 1956—

● = 2, 3, and 4 visits

Risalpur ○   ● Abbotabad
Peshawar   ● Naushera
             ○ Murree
             ● Rawalpindi
Sargoda   ○ Jhelum
           ○ Sialkot
Lahore ● ○ Amritsar
      Jullunda ●   ● Simla
○ Quetta   Ludhiana ●   ● Mussoori
           Ambala ○   ● Dehra Dun
           Patiala ● Roorkee
           Saharanpur ● ● Naini Tal
           ● Delhi
      ○ Pilani   Gurgoan ○
           ○ Aligarh
      ● Jaipur   ● Agra   ● Lucknow
○ Nawabsha   Ajmer ●   Cawnpore   ○ Gorakpur   Darjeeling ●
○ Tando Adam   ○
Karachi ● ○ Hyderabad   Jhansi
           Udaipur ○   Allahabad ○   ● Patna
           Ahmedabad ○   Jabalpur ○   ○ Ramgarh
           ○ Baroda   ○ Indore   Dhanbad ○
                                Asansol ○   ● Burnpur
                      ● Nagpur   Ranchi ●   ○ Santiniketan
           ● Surat   Tata Naga ●   ● Calcutta
           ● Nausari
           ● Deolali   Cuttack ○
Bombay ● ● Panchgani
          ● Poona   Hyderabad ○

~ 879 ~

PERFORMANCES OF

OTHELLO
THE MERCHANT OF VENICE
HAMLET
THE TAMING OF THE SHREW
MACBETH
ROMEO AND JULIET
TWELFTH NIGHT
ARMS AND THE MAN
PYGMALION
SHE STOOPS TO CONQUER
THE SCHOOL FOR SCANDAL
THE IMPORTANCE OF
BEING EARNEST
GASLIGHT
'CHARLIE'S AUNT
THE TEMPEST

Mysore ●   ● Madras
Ootacamund ○
Coimbatore ○

DIRECTOR OF PRODUCTION
Geoffrey Kendal

— PATRONS —
THE RT. HON. COUNTESS
MOUNTBATTEN OF BURMA,
C.L.G.B.E., D.C.V.O.
HIS HIGHNESS THE MAHARAJA
SAHIB BAHADUR OF JAIPUR,
RAJPRAMUKH OF RAJASTHAN
JAIPUR
HIS EXCELLENCY
DR. K.M. MUNSHI, B.A., L.L.B.,
D.LITT., L. ED. GOVERNOR OF
UTTAR PRADESH

---

refund and leave. They said they had come to see him perform and would see the play without him speaking his lines. So Prithviraj mimed his part while the others around him performed normally. The love of the people in the hall gave him enough strength to pull through the show that day.

On the evening of 10 April 1960, *Pathan* was being staged to a packed house in Shrirampur. As the curtain came down to thundering applause, Prithviraj wrote that he felt every bone in his body being pounded with hammers.

At the end of the applause, he quietly announced, 'This is the last performance of my life in theatre.'

SHASHI KAPOOR SAYS, 'WHEN PAPAJI closed down Prithvi Theatres, he hoped to have a small theatre of his own some day. That's how Prithvi Theatre eventually came into being. In the 16 years of Prithvi Theatres, the company never had a base—a theatre with good acoustics, backstage arrangements, proper lighting. He believed that one day he would have a theatre with all these facilities.'

After the last show of Prithvi Theatres, all its belongings—sets, props, costumes—were moved from the Royal Opera House to Kooka Gymkhana in the suburbs. Kooka Gymkhana has long been supplanted by an apartment complex.

Prithviraj saw two plots in the verdant, peaceful Janki Kutir, in Juhu, by the sea and fell in love with the place. This was much before the real estate boom in Mumbai, and Juhu with its coconut groves and fishing shacks was still distant and exotic, not the upmarket, crowded suburb that it has become today. In 1962, Prithviraj leased the two plots from the owner Ram Krishna Bajaj (Kaifi and Shaukat Azmi were his next-door neighbours). It was a very expensive deal. His sons tried to reason with him, 'Papaji, why spend so much on a ten-year lease?' And he would just say, 'You drink foreign whisky and smoke foreign cigarettes, I drink Indian whisky and smoke bidis ... This is my *nasha* (addiction). Ten years is a very long time.'

He passed away exactly ten years later in 1972.

ON ONE OF THE PLOTS A SHED WAS erected to store Prithvi Theatres' belongings, and on the other, a homely little shack—Papaji's Prithvi Jhopda—which remained more or less intact, till 2000, when a multi-storeyed building was constructed in its place.

Both the simple structures were designed by an American lady, a Mrs Contractor, whose husband lived in Janki Kutir.

'When he leased these plots in 1962,' says Shashi, 'he would tell us that it was necessary to have a permanent place for the theatre that would be economically viable, not just for actors, but producers, playwrights—anybody connected with the theatre including the audience; there should be a comfortable place for actors, space to store costumes and sets, a good stage, not hot, so that the actors would not sweat off their make-up, good lights and acoustics.'

Prithvi Jhopda became a meeting ground for actors, including some ex-Prithvi

Shakespeareana on tour—a teenaged Jennifer with her father Geoffrey Kendal (standing).

troupers. They would drop by, chat, and reminisce.

At the time when the company was closed down, the troupe had already started rehearsing for two new plays that never made it to the stage—*Tipu Sultan* and *Ashoka*. Shashi Kapoor's elder son was named Kunal after Emperor Ashoka's son.

PRITHVIRAJ KAPOOR'S VOICE DETERIORAT-ed further, and in 1971 he was diagnosed with Hodgkin's Disease. Around the same time, tragically, his wife too was suffering from galloping cancer.

Shashi Kapoor says, 'I was shooting for *Siddharth* and I had to be away from Bombay for long spells. I knew both my parents were very ill. Then, in April 1972, I had to go to England for three to four weeks to dub for the film, and sought their permission to leave with my family.'

In England, Shashi Kapoor and Jennifer spent their free evenings watching plays. On one such evening, in the middle of a play at the Old Vic, Shashi Kapoor got a call at the theatre. In those days, getting an overseas call through wasn't as effortless as it is today. It was a tedious and time-consuming process—one had to book a call and wait. A sudden call from India must have been like a bolt from the blue. If someone had taken the trouble to get through to London and trace him down to the theatre, the matter had to be serious. Shashi Kapoor's heart thumped wildly as he rushed to take the call. Even though Prithviraj had been ailing, and the worst was to be expected, it still took nerves of steel to give and receive bad news. As the baby of the family, Shashi Kapoor had always been very close to his father. That he was so far away at such a time added to his anguish.

He recalls, 'I really don't know how they got through. Bhabhiji (Krishna Raj Kapoor) and Chintu (Rishi Kapoor) spoke to me. They said Papaji was very ill and that I was to leave for home immediately. I took the next flight out with Jennifer and the children. For once, the 10-hour-long journey seemed to be never-ending. We got in early morning on 29 May. Daboo (Randhir Kapoor) was on the tarmac . . . it was unheard of. We drove straight to Tata Hospital. Papaji was breathing his last.'

It was as if Prithviraj was living on borrowed time, trying to keep death at bay till he could see his youngest son one last time.

'By the time I arrived at the hospital, the doctors had removed all the life-support systems. There were so many people there, including the governor Ali Yavar Jung. When Papaji heard the door open, he quickly turned . . . Rajji told me later that he had been unable to move for a while now. But when he sensed my presence, he managed to move his head. He had a faint smile on his face. I sat by his side, held his hand . . . a couple of hours later he was gone.

'The night before, the doctors had told the family that it was over, but he had survived the whole night when Rajji whispered in his ear that Shashi is coming . . . Shashilala is what Papaji always called me.'

From that day in 1972, Shammi Kapoor didn't shave, till in 2003 when he was taken critically ill and had to be shaved in hospital.

Exactly 16 days later, on 14 June 1972, Rama Kapoor passed away.

'I was very disturbed by my dad and mum passing away,' says Shashi Kapoor. 'After their demise, I realized that I had been working for the past 12 years, and not always in films I was happy about. So around 1975, when it just got too much, I told my wife that I wanted to do something different. And she said, "Why don't you do something that you want to do?" I said, "I would like to make a film," and she said, "Make it." Then I said I also wanted to build a theatre, and she just laughed. But till his last days, Papaji nurtured the dream of building a theatre, and I wanted to fulfil that dream. I wanted to build a theatre at the very spot where he would have wanted to build it.'

ZOHRA SEGAL HAD ONCE ASKED Prithviraj Kapoor why he had named his company Prithvi Theatres—in the plural. He had replied that it was his dream to have a theatre in every town in India.

On 5 November 1978, Prithvi Theatre was inaugurated on the little plot of land where once stood the Prithvi Theatres shed opposite the Prithvi Jhopda.

Over the next 25 years this little haven which came about as a result of the union of two great institutions—Prithvi Theatres and Shakespeareana—was to become a cultural landmark in Mumbai.

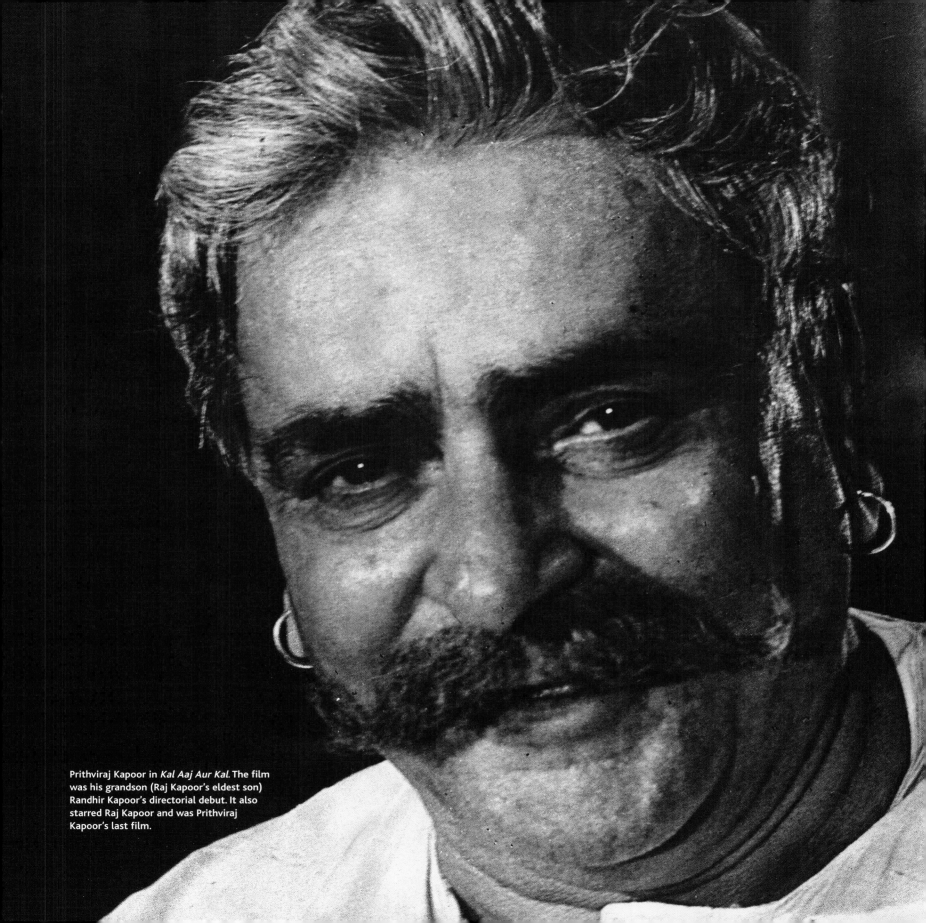

Prithviraj Kapoor in *Kal Aaj Aur Kal*. The film was his grandson (Raj Kapoor's eldest son) Randhir Kapoor's directorial debut. It also starred Raj Kapoor and was Prithviraj Kapoor's last film.

Actors from Telluride Theatre Company from the US, and Footsbarn Travelling Theatre, a travelling theatre troupe, based in France, preparing before a show.

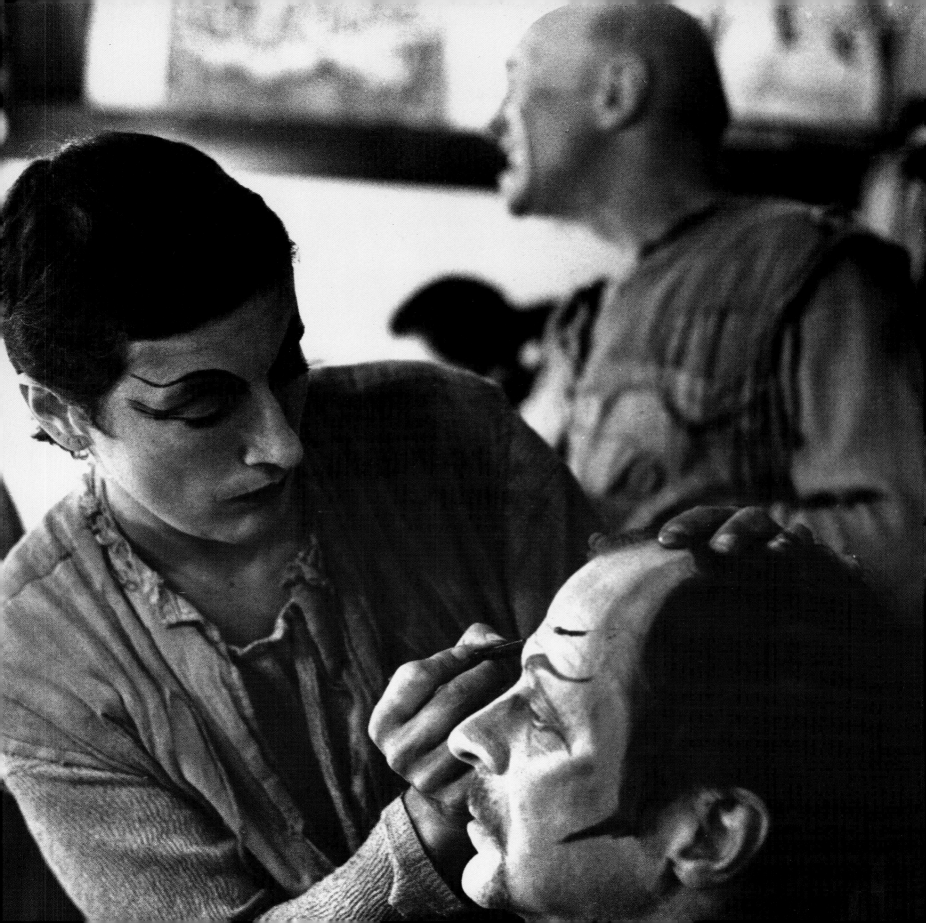

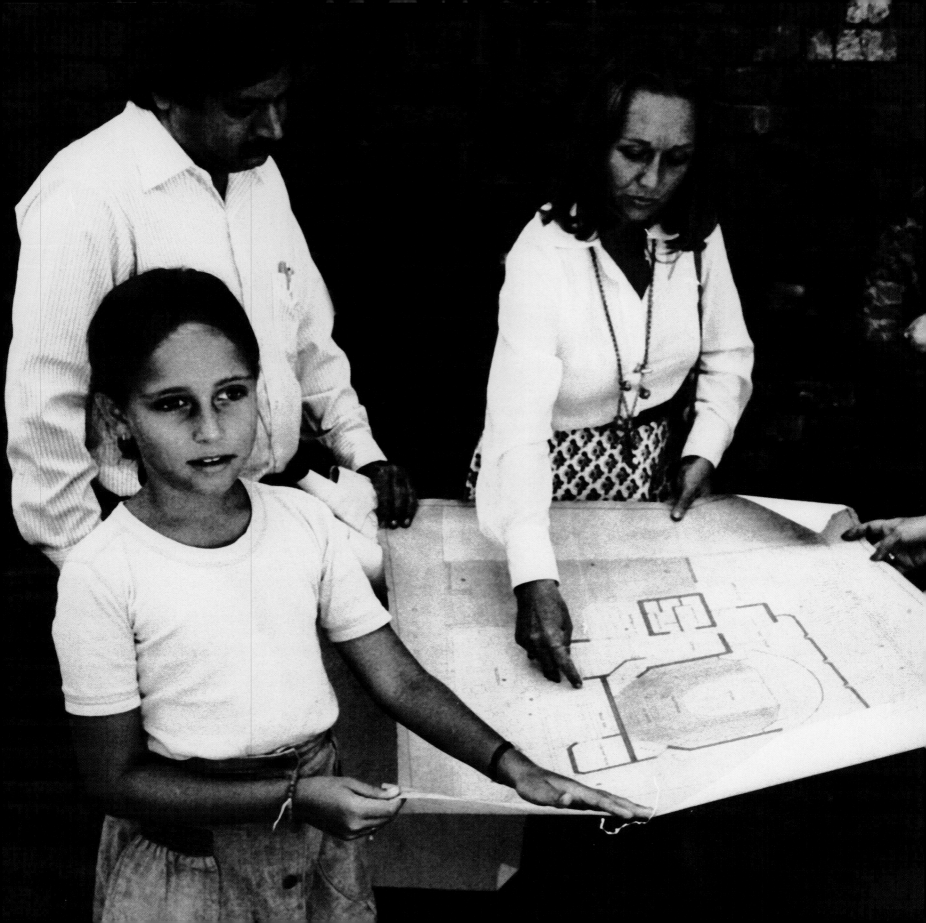

Act II

Scene 1: Prithvi Theatre

THE 10-YEAR LEASE ON the two plots in Juhu expired in 1972—the year Prithviraj passed away. In 1974 Shashi Kapoor bought the two plots and set up the Shri Prithviraj Kapoor Memorial Trust. In a letter to her sister, Felicity Kendal, in London, Jennifer Kapoor wrote, 'Shashi is mad, he wants to build a theatre.'

Later, in an interview, Jennifer said: 'Back in 1962, when the shed was constructed, the idea was to use it for rehearsals and even performances. But it was extremely badly designed. An L-shaped auditorium was hardly the best option for rehearsals, let alone performances.'

Having acquired the plots, Shashi Kapoor started looking around to raise some funds for the trust. After films like *Deewar* and *Trishul,* his film career was flourishing and he did not mind putting in some money of his own into building Prithvi Theatre. Many of his film industry friends got together as well to raise funds. This may well have started the trend of star shows that are such a rage today.

'An organization in Siliguri was willing to donate a little bit of money to the trust, if I could get hold of some stars for a show there,' recalls Shashi Kapoor. 'Those were the days when stars came together for a cause, not for money. Amongst others, Amitabh Bachchan, Rekha, Daboo (Randhir Kapoor), Shekhar Kapur, Shabana Azmi, Mohammad Rafi, Hemant Kumar, Sulakshana Pandit, agreed to participate. The show went on for two days—it was a musical show, what one called a "star nite". Over 18,000 people flocked to see the stars—such a thing had never happened before in Siliguri!'

Mohammad Rafi, Hemant Kumar and Krishna (actress Rani Mukherji's mother) performed on the first day and were scheduled to leave the next day by the noon

'Look after it,' I told her. 'You will have to create it, nurse it.'

SHASHI KAPOOR TO JENNIFER

flight. Sulakshana Pandit was to arrive in the morning to perform on the second day. For some reason Sulakshana missed her flight. Everyone panicked. If a solution was not found quickly, perhaps the show would have to be cancelled. Shashi Kapoor's secretary Shaktilal Vaid, begged Mohammad Rafi to stay back. The singer graciously agreed and saved the day.

This was one of the earliest occasions when Amitabh Bachchan sang and danced, and interacted with the audience. He performed *Mere angne mein tumhara kya kam hai* with Rekha—the folk song was later used in the film *Laawaris* and became a chartbuster. To date this song remains a favourite with Amitabh Bachchan for his stage shows.

'There were two other similar events but not for Prithvi Theatre. One was a function in Pune to promote small savings for which Amitabh, Zeenat and I had gone. The other was a cricket match in Calcutta—Sanjeev Kumar, Vinod Khanna and Randhir Kapoor had also come along,' says Shashi Kapoor nostalgically. 'Amitabh was very negative about the whole thing, he kept saying no one will come, it will be a flop.

'We were staying at Grand Hotel, and from his suite you could see Eden Garden at a distance. Early in the morning at 6, he knocked on my door. It was a misty Calcutta morning. We had tea and again he grumbled that the event would be a washout. After

about an hour, I went to the balcony and saw people coming into the stadium in thousands, like little ants. I called him to the balcony. Unable to believe his eyes, he said, "Are you sure they are coming for the match?" I said, "Of course!"

'That day, we played to a packed stadium of forty to fifty thousand people.'

THOSE WERE THE DAYS, IN THE MID TO late '70s, when Shashi Kapoor had started a new phase of his career—playing 'parallel hero', and doing multiple shifts.

Raj Kapoor was planning *Satyam Shivam Sundaram* (1977) and many leading men wanted to work with the great showman. Raj Kapoor, however, wanted Shashi to play the lead. It was one of the busiest periods of Shashi's career, but even so he told Shaktilal Vaid to take a new diary, put it down in front of Rajji and let him take as many dates as he wanted. The film was meant to have been a quickie, to be completed in three months' flat.

'Shakti came back in tears. Rajji had taken all the dates already allotted to other producers. He also insisted that on the days I was to shoot with him, I wouldn't shoot with anyone else. To accommodate Rajji, I had to work round the clock, doing four to five shifts a day, and sleeping in the car. Rajji promptly nicknamed me "taxi", a sobriquet that was immediately picked up by the press.'

Shashi was seldom around when his dream theatre was being built. He was away for long spells during the first few years of its growth, because of his grinding work schedule.

People thought it strange that he should be investing a large sum of money in a theatre. At that time, there was really no professional Hindi theatre in Mumbai. The Indian People's Theatre Association (IPTA) was fairly active performing social plays; Satyadev Dubey was doing experimental work in Chhabildas Hall; sporadic amateur theatre activities were organized in schools and during religious functions.

Sceptics said nobody would come to Shashi's theatre because it was located in a residential area in suburban Juhu. In those days it was not easy to commute to Juhu. Before the film stars started moving in, Juhu Beach was just a picnic spot even for the people of Mumbai.

Preceding page 62: Jennifer Kapoor and architect Ved Segan working on the plans of Prithvi Theatre. Also seen in the picture is Sanjna Kapoor, aged 9.

Facing page: Jennifer and Shashi Kapoor seated inside Prithvi Theatre waiting for the performance to begin. They always bought tickets for every play they saw.

Shashi Kapoor recalls, 'The government did not know how to handle something like this. They had never given permission for a public building which was not quite public—in the sense that it was a private theatre. We had to bully people for permissions. My cousin, Vicky Kapoor, who was a lawyer, helped us through the legal tussles.'

When Shashi Kapoor had first come up with the idea of setting up a theatre, the then governor, Ali Yavar Jung, had offered him land in the Bandra Reclamation Area (where the Rang Sharda Hotel and auditorium now stand).

Architect Ved Segan had designed actress Raakhee's house, which Shashi and Jennifer had liked very much. So they invited him to design the interiors of Shashi's film production company, Film-valas, in Worli, and subsequently, Prithvi Theatre.

Says Ved, 'The original plan was to demolish the existing structure used for storage, plus a portion built for rehearsals, then build a basement, workshop, cafeteria, and a 200-capacity theatre as a stop-gap measure till the Bandra land was allotted. Ali Yavar Jung proposed a committee be set up to study the proposal. Then we decided not to have a third party involved in the project, and to do it the way we wanted to. Jennifer also thought that once the government came into the picture, the project would

inside walls and create a space for performances. This was a simple and cost-effective solution.'

'We were not doing all this just for Hindi theatre,' says Shashi. 'Jennifer and I just wanted to have a professional theatre. So we built the theatre in such a way that it would attract and encourage people to get involved with theatre. We worked on the basic *dhancha* (framework) of the theatre together, and decided to see what we could do with it.

'Thereafter I was not really involved in the actual making of the theatre. I just looked after the finances, so the entire credit of translating Papaji's dream into reality goes to Jennifer and Ved Segan. The understanding between Jennifer and me was that while it was my idea to build the theatre, it was to be her baby. "Look after it," I told her. "You will have to create it, nurse it." At times, she would get annoyed and say that I had thrust this thing on her. But I think eventually she was quite happy.

'People said it was an ego trip to have a theatre—who knows, perhaps they were right. Be that as it may, I am proud that we were able to build the theatre in spite of very little money coming in from other sources, like the star shows, or a few of my father's contemporaries and friend's like actor Mubarak Merchant. Thanks to my films, I was able to put in most of the money myself. I'm just glad that I could afford to fulfil my father's dream.'

take much longer to get off the ground. Meanwhile, I suggested that we change the roof of the existing structure in Juhu, forego the idea of demolishing the walls, put up a stage, and see people's reaction. Let people use it and see how it goes. It would cost about a lakh. Jennifer liked the idea and that's how we started restructuring the building.'

Jennifer who was never happy with the earlier design, was quoted as having said, 'Even as a store, the building was a failure. After Papaji died most of the costumes, some quite elaborate, and the props, had to be thrown away—the monsoons and the rats had reduced them to a useless heap. Shashi declared that one day he would build a theatre without a screen or projector, and which would be used only for live drama . . . After the Shri Prithviraj Kapoor Memorial Trust was set up, Prithivi Jhopda was partly renovated and rebuilt. There were many ideas for the existing shed—it could be redesigned as a theatre school, or a house for old actors, or perhaps a housing complex with a theatre, a library, a dubbing studio—but finally, we decided to simply cover the old structure with a new roof, remove all the

Scene II: Taking Shape

SHASHI KAPOOR HAD SEEN his father's troupe perform in primitive conditions. With Shakespeareana, Jennifer and the Kendal family did productions designed to be put on anywhere—in classrooms, on board ships, and once, according to theatre lore, actually on a billiards table. So between them, Jennifer and Shashi knew exactly what they wanted the new Prithvi Theatre to be.

Jennifer arranged for Ved Segan to travel around Europe and England to see different kinds of theatres. He had never been involved with theatre design earlier, or exposed to the kind of theatre he got to see in England, and the experience was thrilling for him.

'At no stage did we discuss how this theatre was to be designed,' says Segan. 'After Jennifer and I returned from England, she asked me what I had come up with. I told her Young Vic in London. "That's exactly what I had in mind," she said.'

The original plan had been to make a temporary theatre until the actual one got built—but enthusiasm got the better of Jennifer and Segan. She said in an interview, 'Step by unplanned step, we found we were actually building our "ideal" theatre— soundproofed, air-conditioned, comfortable, well-equipped. Not so simple and not so cheap either!'

Thinking back now, Segan says, 'The essence of architecture lies in the concept. Even though the general belief is that the architect is concerned only with the physical, not the conceptual, the dream of the client and the concept of the architect have to coincide. If they are not in tune then even if you spend crores, things don't happen. This building has love, affection, and the complete involvement of the client. Jennifer had the ability to make things happen, to make the people feel that they had made it happen. She could take people along.'

What must have helped the creative process along was the absence of any 'committees' or organization to deal with. Says Segan, 'It was a person-to-person contact all the way through. Shashi and Jennifer acted in unison. I was directly in touch with Jennifer, and Shashi never interfered. People asked if I had done a theatre before. If you are sensitive to space, colour, form, it hardly matters

what functionality the building is put to.

'As an architect, I give more importance to the concept and to the person who is going to use it, than to my individual style. Each design is therefore different. What matters immensely is how a client communicates his needs. Shashi and Jennifer knew their requirements.'

To begin with, the only requirement was to build a theatre which would be inexpensive enough for companies to be able to put up professional productions without worrying about the rent. And professional— not commercial—was the keyword. Jennifer firmly believed that if people wanted to experiment, they could do that at home or in private, and come to the theatre only when they were fully ready to show there work to an audience. Theatre was not a 'hobby' for either Shashi or Jennifer, but something to be taken seriously and treated with respect. 'Theatre should be practised only by those who are willing to make it their life's work,' Jennifer felt strongly, 'and not an after-hours hobby.'

Jennifer hoped that Prithvi Theatre would provide a challenge and the right stimulus to talent which in turn would enrich the performing arts—films, theatre, music; that

Facing page: Architect Ved Segan, stands under a mask of Prithviraj Kapoor, outside Prithvi Theatre. This mask mysteriously disappeared from the wall one day.

it would inspire people to work in the theatre with dedication; that this little theatre would spark off a whole new enthusiasm for live entertainment. 'We will have everything here, music, dance, drama, poetry, everything but weddings,' she said.

Plans of renovating the old storage shed into a theatre space with minimal expense had to be abandoned. The walls had been made during severe cement shortage in the '70s, and a kind of lime used that absorbed water—a major problem in a seaside location. To pull down these walls and rebuild new ones in the same place did not make sense. From the initial estimate of one lakh, the expenses just escalated.

Segan recalls, 'Jennifer and I would meet everyday, with Shashi joining us whenever he could, and each time, a new addition would come up. We thought of having steel girders on the outside, because they had salvage value—after all this was meant to be a temporary structure. When the theatre was near completion, Shashi said, "What about acoustics?" The demands started growing. The biggest challenge was roofing. Since asbestos cement sheets would not stop the sound from travelling outside the building, we had to use pre-cast concrete panels.'

Shashi Kapoor had started Film-valas around 1976-77, the same time that Prithvi was being built. Their first production, Junoon, directed by Shyam Benegal was underway, and funds were short.

Shashi Kapoor remembers, 'The theatre was an unusual kind of construction and it looked as though it would take a hundred years to complete. I was fed up. I had made

Jennifer Kapoor's Jottings on Theatre Design:

Why are forms other than the orthodox stage demanded?

The answer from practitioners to enthusiasts is that they develop a more direct relation between an actor and the audience. The actor ceases to be part of a picture to be looked at, and is instead embraced by the audience. The actor becomes essential both psychologically and physically because everyone must be brought near. Inevitably this means a stage thrust out into the audience, or one which is completely surrounded by them.

Definitive advice for both these encompassed forms: Keep the stage area small and do not allow actors and audience to use the same entrance into the auditorium. Also, the stage area must be low or it will be impossible to light (unclear) without a glare in the eyes of the audience. One must keep the 'Actors World and the Real World' together but strictly separate.

Beware of the multiple frame(s): It is suitable for everything, good for nothing.

A well-designed auditorium will gather the audience together and at the same time focus attention on a particular area of the stage. This area is referred to as the actor's 'point of command', which everyone in the audience can see and where all the important action transpires.

In a badly designed auditorium the members of the audience do not feel gathered-up and directed. Rather they become separate groups or form a large group, which goes ragged and falls apart towards the edges, so to speak.

Today it is the forms of theatre, which aim at the greatest contact between the actor and his audience, which could run the greatest risk of misplacing the focus. One such form is the thrust stage in which the audience sits on three sides of the acting area. The fourth side being reserved for a permanent background.

It is better to decide on a form and make it as flexible as possible rather than adaptable to two or more forms.

The open-end stage is good when it is there because everyone recognizes that a proscenium would merely be an encumbrance on the site. There is no point in having a proscenium under conditions where its main advantages—wing space and overhead flying— are reduced to a mere token due to lack of space and money. Once the stage width has been restricted to that of the auditorium, the open stage will provide a better formula. The forthright recognition of limitations will provide a discipline which acts as a stimulus to artistic invention. This spirit replaces the vexation, which could come from a cramped, incomplete stage. This results in the 'why-did-they-not-give-us-enough-space' attitude.

There are theatre pundits who pronounce that for 'theatre' to survive (they do not equate this with 'audience') everyone must be jammed together on hard benches or even sit on the floor. The same pundits show no sign of doing such a thing themselves.

The first and greatest difficulty is, we will have to get directors and designers to conceptualize sculpturally, that is, three dimensionally instead of picture-wise, two dimensionally. Most directors and virtually all designers think in terms of visual images. Such images are almost invariably seen from one viewpoint and that viewpoint is from the centre front. This is a deeply ingrained habit of mind, which is most difficult to overcome.

This difficulty does not exist for an actor, who usually, once he has surrendered himself to the feeling of being surrounded or nearly surrounded by his audience, finds great imaginative stimulus from the freedom, to play directly, instead of having to present a false, unchanging face to the audience, as in proscenium theatre.

In terms of an open stage, one has bandied about such words as 'intimacy', 'audience participation' and 'involvement'. Herein it is tempting, once the old barrier of the proscenium arch has been removed, to go further and to spill over any boundary line that may remain between the audience and actor. However, practical experience suggests it is important to maintain a clear line of demarcation and that when an actor oversteps it, the result tends to be one of embarrassment and unease among the audience. At such times, the effect is to alienate rather than involve.

What about the relationship of audience and actor, the form of the theatre? Is a theatre, which is adaptable to two different forms, twice as effective or not half as effective? We believe the latter is the case. The design of a single form is so difficult that seldom can we say the job is absolutely successful. Adaptability is compromise and man is never stimulated by compromise. Decide on the form of theatre you want and then stick to it.

Representational scenery, placed upon the stage by the designer for the purpose of making a visual statement, to say the least, is not appropriate to the open stage. The open stage may be most effective when scenery in the accepted sense is reduced to an absolute minimum or even dispensed with entirely. The effect of the special relationship between, for instance, a number of known and carefully placed items of furniture can be most evocative provided the audience can see the whole stage floor, and is, therefore, made aware of such a relationship. It would seem the designer's prime function in an open stage is the organization of space rather than the filling of it with decoration.

About Prithvi, let us not pretend we have not made enormous blunders. Every company which performs here will have its pet complaints, some of which we will have to take seriously enough to make changes later. But let us prevent the theatre we intended to build to be perfectly meshed—without shabby curtains, and no ill-trained people around. Let us hope companies will use it in its ideal way, with the minimum of scenery, and cameo sets, within the area available. Or let us hope that eventually it will be used as a producing theatre with every production specially designed for this particular space.

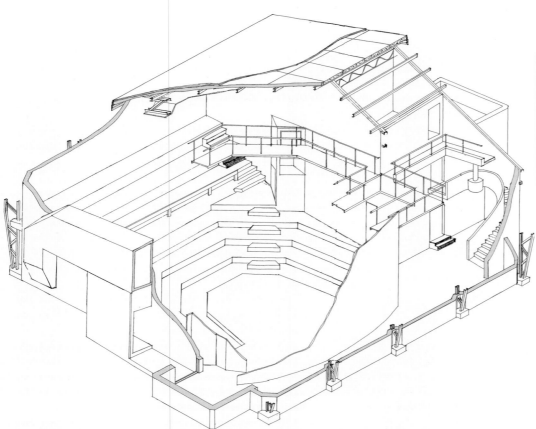

Preceding pages 70-71: Ved Segan's impressions of Prithvi Theatre.

Left: Ved Segan's section sketches for the interior and the exterior (facing page) of Prithvi Theatre.

disturbances while a play was on, no one walking in and out and a 'strictly no latecomers' policy which still stands, despite fights and tantrums from theatregoers, and some actors even threatening to boycott the theatre.

At one point, differences cropped up between Jennifer and Shashi over the height of the stage. He wanted it to be 12 inches, while she wanted eight. So a mock stage was built—with one half built according to Shashi's specifications and the other half as Jennifer preferred it. Eight inches it was.

'Many major decisions were made in this slaphappy way. Luckily we had an architect who actually enjoyed this. In fact, I think the theatre has ended up being a very personal thing for the three of us—Ved, Shashi and me,' Jennifer said in an interview.

'Then Shashi dropped the biggest bombshell,' says Segan. 'He wanted the theatre to be air-conditioned. We had not designed the building with air-conditioning in mind. Instead, it had plenum extraction— there were vents on one side and exhaust fans on the other so that air would circulate and voices would carry. In the end, we did come up with a solution—the air-conditioning ducts are outside now.'

a full-length film and the theatre was still not ready! *Junoon* was not a joke. It had a big star cast, sets, war scenes. I had to put my foot down and tell Jennifer and Segan to complete the theatre soon.'

Segan reminisces, 'Getting the acoustics right for the theatre meant an additional budget of Rs 35,000-40,000. And there was just no more money. Shashi said to just go ahead and open the theatre without acoustics. But how could we do that? Jennifer gave Rs 5000 from her kitchen money . . . We used glass wool waste and wood from the sets . . . all on-the-spot improvisations.'

Both Prithvi Theatres and Shakespeareana had spent years staging plays in school and college halls, or in cinema houses with very poor acoustics. So Shashi and Jennifer were really keen that the voice of the actor be given top priority. A story that had become a legend in the family was about Laura Liddel's performance as Portia in *Merchant of Venice* in Singapore. When she uttered the famous lines, 'Falleth as the gentle rain from heaven', there was a torrential outburst of rain upon the corrugated tin roof of the theatre which made the entire audience guffaw with laughter. Shashi never wanted to have a repeat of such a thing in his brand new theatre—he said in an interview that he couldn't bear the thought of the rain going *'pit pit'* on the roof.

'Give the actor what the actor needs, give the audience what the audience needs,' was his philosophy. Which meant no

When it was finally ready, the 200-seater Prithvi Theatre, with its octagonal 'thrust' stage—a stage that jutted out into the audience, with seating on three sides—had perfect acoustics—even a whisper could be heard in the last row—and a comfortable, welcoming ambience. Segan explains, 'We were somewhat lucky to have naturally quiet surroundings. The use of thick masonry walls for the hall, pre-stressed pre-cast concrete slabs for the roof and properly insulated Plaster of Paris false ceilings took care of the acoustics. To cut down the noise of the air-conditioning unit, specially designed silencers were included in the ducts. Our thrust stage itself brought the audience quite near the acting area. The carefully calculated volume of the hall contained the sound energy generated long enough and the profile of the roof itself helped us in deflecting the sound to the desired places. The sound absorption panels are designed to give the most suitable reverberation time for speech, or by turning them over, for music.'

People who dropped by to see the theatre while it was under construction, wondered what kind of theatre it was. There were no curtains, nor did it have a proscenium stage! What would one do with the dead bodies, a theatrewallah wondered! Jennifer replied that this was the need of the day. 'Tomorrow if a proscenium

theatre is needed, I will demolish this and build another theatre. When people watch an accident on the street, do they stand in a straight line?' she said defending the concept of the thrust stage with audiences seated on three sides. She had anticipated that the very shape of the stage would do away with the need for heavy scenery and props, which in turn would keep the cost of production low—an advantage for new groups with limited budgets.

Segan recalls, 'People said that Prithvi was a western concept, that some foreigner had designed it. That did upset Jennifer. "When will we appreciate our own people?" she said. She even said in a television interview that the theatre was designed by an Indian. Actually, it's not a western concept, it's universal. Even tribals had this kind of theatre, where the audience was seated around the performing area.'

For Segan, successful theatre is when

the world of the actor unites with the world of the audience. When the curtain between the two is removed, the two distinct worlds of the actor and the audience form a continuum, with the same elements of light, shade, form, space, colours binding them together.

'Would this building have been successful were it not Prithvi Theatre? I believe that Prithvi Theatre works very well because it does not have a strong personality. Just as water takes the form of the vessel it is poured into, Prithvi Theatre takes on the form of the play that is being staged in it. Often buildings overpower you. The scale of Prithvi Theatre is such that you accept it and it accepts you. I am not surprised at the response this theatre has got from the audience and performers. Other theatres have more money, but this has something extra. What that is, I really don't know . . .'

Finally towards the end of 1978, Prithvi Theatre was ready. IPTA's *Bakri*, a political satire, was scheduled to open the theatre on 3 November—Prithviraj Kapoor's birth

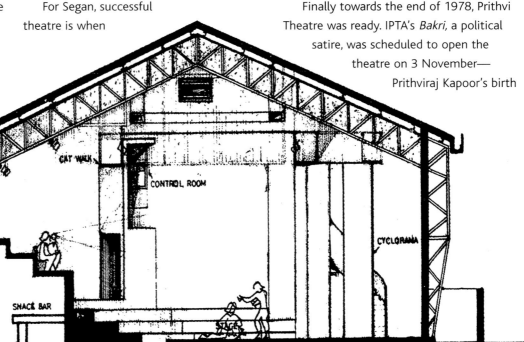

The Prithvi Theatre

Left, right and facing page extreme left: Work in progress at the Prithvi Theatre.

Centre below: Lightman Bhagu Patel who has been with Prithvi Theatre since its inception in 1978.

Below right: Footsbarn actors in the greenroom.

Below extreme right: Outside the newly constructed Prithvi Theatre, Satyadev Dubey (back to camera), Amrish Puri, Sunil Shanbag, Kiran Vairale and Sunila Pradhan.

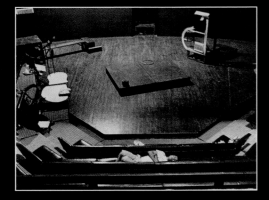

LIGHTING: Catwalk: at 18'6" height following the profile of the thrust stage and parallel to the end stage. Light control room—to the front of the house. Stage lighting: 40 lamps with 24 dimmers.

STAGE: Open thrust: width 20 feet (provision for 28 feet) depth 16 feet.
End stage: Width 40 feet, depth 16 feet.

DRESSING ROOMS: 4 on the upper floor level to accommodate 14 dressing tables (provision for extra if necessary).

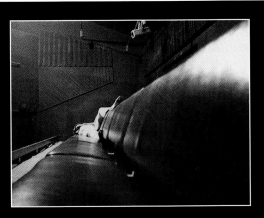

ENTRANCE FOYER: 40'X14' to be used as an art gallery when show is not on.

STRUCTURE: The main auditorium has steel portals with prestressed, precast RCC roofing, while the rest is load bearing with RCC roof.

AUDITORIUM: 39'x39' comfortably padded benches seating approximately 225, capacity to accommodate more as seats are not numbered.

Dharamsey (Stage Manager)

Complete control, responsibility of maintenance etc. of all lighting, sound, scenery, back-stage furniture, — management of back-stage personnel.

Maintenance of all electrical installations on the estate

The supervision of the A/C plant maintenance

Theatre Manager

Co-ordinating between the various depts of the Theatre. — E of the Theatre with the Trust. Receiving & replying to all mail-applications for dates. In the absence of the Trustees, the allotment of dates & cancellation dates. The allotment of rehearsal dates (technical rehearsals in consultation with the stage-management). The control of front of house staff. The control of the board display, — the notifications to the press. Organising publicity etc. for any shows presented by

Occasional meetings with the Trustees to discuss changes in policy or programme. Giving reports on all new companies & productions to the Trustees. In some cases reading the scripts of new plays.

Collectively working towards establishing a fund to help subsidize the theatre.

Jennifer Kendal's instructions to Prithvi Theatre's staff in her own handwriting.

Facing page: Jottings from Shashi Kapoor's diary after his performance with Shakespeareana at the Waltair University Theatre. Till this day he recalls the splendid design of this theatre.

anniversary—because Kaifi Azmi, then President of IPTA and Prithviraj's neighbour in Janki Kutir felt this would be an honour for IPTA.

It came as a shock when a week before the opening day, M.S. Sathyu, the director of *Bakri*, said he was not ready with the play. So, on 5 November, two days later, Majma performed G.P. Deshpande's *Uddhwasta Dharmashala*, directed by Om Puri. The list of actors was impressive—Om Puri himself, Naseeruddin Shah, Karan Razdan, Rohini Hattangady, Neelam Mansingh Chowdhary, Suhas Khandke and Naresh Suri.

The show was a hit, and Prithvi Theatre had finally taken wing! At that point, it was called Prithvi Theatre Workshop because everyone still hoped that a bigger, better structure would soon replace it. No one foresaw that it would stand tall and proud a quarter century later.

Kapoor had said, 'My hope is that Prithvi Theatre will have a company of its own that will put up productions designed specifically for this stage. Ideally, there would be a company under contract but not necessarily the only one to stage productions, as it would be desirable to stage plays in different languages. But a group of actors could be called upon to stage productions that would run. Surely such a tiny theatre could run a play for two or three weeks. Eventually a repertoire could be built up and part of the time the company could tour leaving the theatre free for music and visiting companies.'

She could not fulfil this ambition, but she did see her 'baby' grow and thrive on the creative energy it infused into Bombay's fledgling theatre circles.

The National School of Drama in Delhi had started disgorging trained actors who came to Bombay with stars in their eyes from the mid '70s on. The ever-active inter-collegiate drama circuit had young hopefuls waiting for an opportunity to showcase their talent to the world. Prithvi Theatre opened up a whole new world of opportunities for these newcomers.

Segan says wistfully, 'Initially, even after the theatre opened to the public, I used to go there every day. Then Satyadev Dubey made a remark, "*Ved, bachcha bada ho jaaye to ungli chhod deni chahiye.*" ' (Ved, when a child grows up, you must let go of its hand.)

PRITHVIRAJ KAPOOR'S MENTOR AND friend Jai Dayal had written, 'Prithvi dreams and his first and fundamental dream is a very solid one—of bricks and mortar. Prithvi wants a theatre—not a theatre in the air but a solid structure on solid soil, a home of his own.'

'I was very happy from the very first day, because this is something people said would never happen and it did,' says Shashi Kapoor.

'When he closed down Prithvi Theatres, he had still hoped to build a theatre. He did try to save money, but couldn't because he had to pay a lot of taxes—the price for being very straight with his income. I started Prithvi Theatre with my father's vision, not my vision. Then Jennifer added her own vision to it. I was just behind her. Finally, it was Jennifer and Ved Segan who built it. You need people who are crazy about theatre to do something like this, it's not just a question of paying salaries. It should be an obsession, a religion.'

Just before the theatre opened, Jennifer

Scene III: Early Days

CONTEMPORARY HINDI theatre in Mumbai can be clearly divided into two phases—pre-Prithvi and post-Prithvi. The pre-Prithvi phase was, as Naseeruddin Shah says, 'hellishly tough'. The few large auditoriums in the city were expensive to rent, and there was no guarantee of an audience—going to the theatre had yet to become a popular evening pastime, and then, as now, the competition from cinema was strong.

The post-Prithvi phase witnessed a flourishing, vigorous theatre, not necessarily financially sound, but constantly attracting new talent into its fold while keeping the adrenalin flowing in the veins of the veterans.

A little before the new Prithvi Theatre started, Mumbai theatre came under the influence of the Chhabildas movement, of which Satyadev Dubey, Amol Palekar, Achyut Vaze, Arvind and Sulabha Deshpande and Rohini Jayadeva Hattangady were the leading lights. A tiny school hall in Dadar—a noisy locality in Central Mumbai—became the crucible for experimental theatre, mostly Marathi, but some Hindi as well.

Spectators sat on the floor or on folding metal chairs, fans whirred noisily overhead, the din of the traffic outside blended with the voices of actors; but the flexibility the space offered, and the low rates of the tickets made this kind of theatre very popular with groups and audiences.

Fledgling theatre groups, however, dreamt of a space which would be attractive, comfortable and inexpensive. Prithvi Theatre was the answer to their prayers.

Word about the new theatre coming up in Juhu soon reached the nearby Mithibai College, then a hotbed of theatre activity with Mahendra Joshi, Shafi Inamdar, Paresh Rawal, Feroz Khan, Naushil Mehta hanging out at its canteen and planning productions for inter-collegiate competitions.

Naushil Mehta says, 'We were in the canteen when someone mentioned that Jennifer Kapoor was building a theatre in Juhu, just round the corner. We were part bewildered, part excited—why would anyone do such a thing? So we went to check it out. The structure was up, but the floor was still not ready. We clapped our hands and heard the echoes, and like know-it-alls, we sniggered at the acoustics. Jennifer heard us and walked up to us. We introduced ourselves and got talking. She wasn't quite sure then of the exact function of the edifice. We being young couldn't believe it could make a huge difference to theatre. Later, we were amazed that it did.'

WITH TYPICAL 'ENGLISH' DISTASTE FOR pomp and show, Prithvi Theatre opened with a minimum of fuss. There were no formal invitation cards, just a few phone calls to family and friends, and to some members of the original Prithvi Theatres.

Today the print media and TV crews would give an arm and a leg to cover such an event. In 1978, when Majma staged the inaugural production of Prithvi Theatre—*Uddhwasta Dharmashala*—the group did not even have money to hire a photographer.

Om Puri, the director of *Uddhwasta Dharmashala*, who also acted in the play recalls, 'All of us from Majma came to know about the theatre. I had done films with Shashiji, so we knew it was being built. Then I approached Jennifer and said that we would like to perform there, and she said, "Yes anytime, it's ready." She didn't want to do anything formal, so we just sent some simple printed letters to as many people we could think of, a few journalists. We had no money for publicity, so we sought Amol Palekar's advice. He directed us to Radical Publicity, and they agreed to put in two small ads about the play in the papers and told us we could pay for them later!

'So on the opening night, lots of people turned up. The write-up on the play was the first ever write-up to appear in the press

Prithvi Theatre Workshop was inaugurated with a Hindi play "Udhwasta Dharamshala" performed by 'Majma', a theatre group, consisting of graduates from the National School of Drama, New Delhi, and the F. T. I. I. of Pune. Snapped at the theatre are. from left, standing : T. C. Puri, Pushvinder Chaudhury, Sharad Joshi, Nasiruddin Shah, Mrs. Jennifer Kapoor, Sanjana Kapoor, (daughter of Shashi Kapoor), Shashi Kapoor, Vikram Malhotra, Suhas, Neelam Chaudhury, Naresh Suri, Roop Kumar and director Om Puri, who directed the play. Squatting on the floor are Yusuf Mehta, Fatima Merchant, Athar Nawaaz, Ajay Gadodia and Madan Jain.

Above: Prithvi Theatre was inaugurated with a show of Majma's *Uddhwasta Dharmashala* written by G.P. Deshpande, with a sterling cast.

Right: Sanjna Kapoor giving flowers to Om Puri after the show of *Uddhwasta Dharmashala as* Neelam Mansingh Chowdhry watches.

about me. People were curious to learn more about the group as well. I loved the theatre. It was so intimate and compact. The actor had to make almost no effort to project his voice. The spectators were seated on three sides of the thrust stage, so you felt you were sitting on their lap and talking to them. The stage didn't cut you off from the audience. It was a wonderful feeling to perform there.'

Uddhwasta Dharmashala was an intense play about a Marxist intellectual, facing an inquiry. Naseeruddin Shah who played one of the men on the board of inquiry, says, 'I don't recall the performance too well, but being in a brand new theatre with so many celebrities in the audience, was a very thrilling experience for us. The play improved greatly after a few shows. I was terribly anxious that the audience shouldn't get bored, because I didn't know what to think of that play myself. I had thought it was a little verbose, so were we going to get hooted off . . . But there is a sardonic sense of humour in the interrogation scenes which the audiences were able to see. I don't think the play in itself made a huge impact but it definitely established Om as an actor.'

Majma was a group of graduates from the National School of Drama, who had come to Mumbai for lack of opportunity elsewhere. They stayed with friends who had come in earlier to try their luck, rehearsed in school halls, churches, on the beach, in buses, trains and dhabas. It was sheer happenstance that Prithvi Theatre came up around the same time, and provided them just the platform they needed.

applause . . . The magic of theatre lies in the fact that a whole lot of people who love each other, who enjoy spending time with each other, share each other's joys and sorrows and dreams, pool in for the same cause, sweat together, struggle together, work together, laugh and cry together—that never happens in a film.

'Of the 100-odd films that I have done, I can think of only four or five where I have had this experience. Filmmaking by its very nature does not permit this kind of camaraderie. I have just not enjoyed the plays that I have done in which I have not been involved in every aspect of the production. Turning up two hours before the show and asking someone for your costume is not my idea of theatre. Without all these friends, Om could not have done the job and he is well aware of it and never failed to acknowledge it. We all did it for love, we couldn't afford to pay anyone a penny. We would lose whatever little money Om earned from the films he was doing in putting up these plays, but we had a ball doing it. Looking back I don't know how we pulled it off . . . but we persevered. I really think it was because we enjoyed each other's company so much. Om and I cemented a friendship at that time that has lasted till today. It has really happened only through our work.'

Naseeruddin Shah, then with Majma, adds, 'Om took the initiative. He said it was our job to get the work ready and present it when the ways and means came our way. That was the philosophy of our group. Suhas Khandke and Karan Razdan were our benefactors; they had homes in Bombay and we were always welcome. Majma couldn't have happened without the love and concern of all these friends. That to me is really the magic of theatre, not the immediate response of the audience nor the

Naseeruddin Shah staged the second play at Prithvi—Eugene Ionesco's *The Lesson*, a play from the French theatre of the absurd about a pupil's visit to the house of a mad professor. The play marked Shah's preference for doing theatre in English. During the five

years that Majma was around, it staged other memorable plays—*Bichchoo, Giddh, Zoo Story, Andhon Ka Haathi*. One of the last things the group did was produce the first shows of the Samuel Beckett masterpiece, *Waiting for Godot*. Later Naseeruddin Shah set up his own company, Motley, along with friends Benjamin Gilani and Tom Alter. Their production of *Waiting for Godot* is one of Motley's longest-running plays. Till date, Naseeruddin Shah remains addicted to theatre.

Gilani wrote about the play, 'The reason why we, at Motley, keep returning to the play, is because we feel that we have grown just a little, matured just a little, begun to "feel" just a little more about Godot with each passing year. And it's not just that. It's also because there is the satisfaction of seeing some of our friends return to see the play, again and again, even as a whole new audience sits in a darkened theatre, and tries to search for an answer to the query which runs almost like a sub-title in the play— "What's all this about?"'

Majma proved to be the launching pad for a lot of actors who made it big on the

silver screen. Om Puri confesses that this had been the idea behind forming the group in the first place. 'What could we show the film producers? I didn't have an impressive personality, nor did I have relatives in the film industry. Had I not done *Bichchoo*—a comedy based on Moliere's *The Scorpion*, I would not have got *Jaane Bhi Do Yaaron*. I did use theatre to get into films, and why not? I was an actor, I had no other qualifications.'

Shashi Kapoor admits that after Prithvi Theatre started, his film company benefited hugely from the talent it threw up, and cast a whole lot of actors from the stage— Amrish Puri, Supriya Pathak, Reema Lagoo, Kulbhushan Kharbanda, Ranjit Kapoor, Neena Gupta, Anupam Kher, amongst others.

A few days after the opening of Prithvi Theatre, M.S. Sathyu was ready with his

production, and *Bakri* was finally staged, and went on to become quite a success. Ramesh Talwar , a well-known film and stage director associated with IPTA, remarks, 'Before Prithvi, we used to count our losses at the end of the year. After Prithvi we made modest profits.'

Satyadev Dubey, who, according to Naseeruddin Shah, single-handedly held aloft the banner of Hindi theatre in the pre-Prithvi days, also shifted his running productions to Prithvi Theatre. Over the next few months, he staged plays like *Accha Ek Baar Phir*, *Aarakt Kshan*, *Apartyashit*, *Abe Bewakoof* and *Arre Mayavi Sarovar* at the theatre.

Sunil Shanbag who started his theatre career with Dubey's Theatre Unit and went on to set up his own group, Arpana, recollects, 'The minute there is a space, things start happening around it. There was genuine experimentation and an audience

ready to be challenged. Jennifer Kapoor tried to make the theatre accessible for audiences and actors. When we got long runs, we lived there. We used to go there on Thursday evening and leave Sunday night. We slept in the foyer or the green room. If we wanted to have a party, we had it at the cottage opposite. Prithvi was like home space. Where else do you have access to every part of the theatre?'

For a few months, Prithvi did not have a licence to sell tickets. So after the performance, the groups used to stand outside with *jholis* much like Prithviraj Kapoor did, to collect money for charity. Om Puri told his Majma team to emulate Prithviraj and his troupe, 'Don't have eye contact with the people . . . don't look up. Let people give whatever they can afford to. Be happy if it's a 100-rupee note. Don't feel unhappy if it is eight annas.'

In the initial days, to encourage groups and audiences to come to Prithvi Theatre, Jennifer decided to charge a rent of just one rupee per ticket. Often the evening's takings

Facing page, (left to right): Deepa Basrur (Lagoo), Amrish Puri, Bhakti Barve, Jyotsna Karyekar and Amol Palekar in a cast picture of Satyadev Dubey's early production of Mohan Rakesh's *Aadhe Adhure*, a landmark play about a dysfunctional family. Dinesh Thakur also did a production of this play many years later.

Facing page, below: A young Satyadev Dubey.

Right: Anupam Kher and Kiron Thakur Singh in Ekjute's *Chandanpur Ki Champabai* (1984), based on Bertolt Brecht's *The Good Woman of Setzuan*. Kiron married Anupam Kher and both are now famous film and TV stars, who occasionally still do theatre.

were just five rupees! 'I didn't agree with the one-rupee-per-ticket-sold rental scheme,' says Om Puri. 'I told Jennifer that it was not practical and it would be misused. Actors would end up using the theatre as a free audition space—they could invite ten film directors to see a play, and give the theatre just ten rupees, and they would do plays not for the audiences, but for film people.'

Prithvi became a nesting place for struggling actors hoping to be discovered by filmmakers. And very often they were. Directors like Shyam Benegal and Govind Nihalani picked a lot of actors from the stage. Anupam Kher's performance as an old man in *Desire Under the Elms*, with Kiron Thakur Singh, later his wife, was instrumental in Mahesh Bhatt offering him the role of an old man in *Saaransh*, the film that launched his film career.

But not everyone used Prithvi merely as a halfway house between stage and screen—there were those who went on to make theatre their career. Three such groups full of young blood—Ank, Yatri and Ekjute—that came into existence because of Prithvi Theatre, have grown with it; others like Vijeta, Bhoomika, Coda dropped out after a while, and yet others like Surnai, and Natak Company keep resurfacing whenever they feel the urge to do theatre.

Dinesh Thakur, a stage actor from Delhi, came to seek his fortune in Mumbai in the early '70s. His group Ank used to perform during Durga Puja and Ganeshotsav and occasionally at Chhabildas Hall. 'After I saw Prithvi, I realized that doing theatre could actually be comfortable. In the initial days, there used to be just 5-6 shows a month. The rest of the time, the theatre was made

available to groups for just five rupees. When Ank staged its first production, Badal Sircar's *Baki Itihaas* in December 1978, there were four or five people in the hall,' he says. Thakur remembers how tough it was in the early days to get people to come to Prithvi Theatre to watch plays. The group members would sell tickets at traffic signals or go from door to door with their booklets. A route-map would be printed behind the ticket, as people did not know where the theatre was! Since Thakur had appeared in a few films by the late '70s, people would buy tickets, but not turn up for the shows.

'We were working with almost a missionary zeal to get people into the theatre. In 1979, Ank held its first festival—six shows of three plays: *Baki Itihaas, Suno Janmajeya, Yeh Sheh Yeh Maat*. There were 20-25 people in each show, the total

Above: Dinesh Thakur (right) and Naresh Suri (left) in *Baki Itihaas*. This play by Badal Sircar was the first to be performed at Prithvi Theatre by Thakur's group Ank.

Middle: Shafi Inamdar and his wife Bhakti Barve in *Ada*, in Hum's Hindi version of the Gujarati hit *Lady Lal Kunwar,* based on an Italian play in which a man's mistress fools him into marrying her.

Below: Vinod Kapoor, Basheer Khan and Lilliput in Yatri's *Ek Tha Gadha*. This play based on a Sharad Joshi satire is one of Om Katare's best about a power-hungry Nawab who mistakenly announces state mourning and a grand funeral for a washerman's donkey. When the error is discovered, a man is killed and dumped into the coffin to save the Nawab's face, and life goes on. The play was a farce but also a serious comment on the wilfulness of those in power.

collection was Rs 135. Shashi and Jennifer came to see all the plays and always bought tickets. After each show Jennifer would come backstage and say, "Don't lose heart, people will come." It was Jennifer and her manager, the popular Dharamsey Merchant's support to the groups that was responsible for the eventual success of Prithvi Theatre.'

Nadira Zaheer Babbar met Shashi Kapoor in Delhi just before Prithvi Theatre opened. She had heard he was building a theatre for IPTA and told him he was doing a very great thing. He smiled and said, 'It's not just for IPTA, it's for everyone.'

When Nadira came to Mumbai towards the end of the '70s, she went to Prithvi Theatre for the first time to see IPTA's *Sufaid Kundali*, an adaptation of Bertolt Brecht's *The Caucasian Chalk Circle*, with Shabana Azmi in the lead role. 'The acoustics were magical,' she says. 'The other special thing about Prithvi was that it seemed like an extension of home. In the air was the spirit of Papaji, it was not a place built for profit, and that purity of intention could be felt. The audience was still thin. When we did *Chandanpur Ki Champabai* (based on *The Good Woman of Setzuan* by Bertolt Brecht), there were more people on stage than in the hall.'

WHEN NADIRA WANTED TO FORM HER own group, Ekjute, in 1979, Jennifer provided not only a stage, but food and accommodation as well. 'I brought down two productions from Delhi, *Lower Depths* and *Yahudi Ki Ladki*. She offered Prithvi Jhopda for the group to stay in. I was

astounded by her generosity. About 27-28 people stayed there, and we saved a packet on accommodation and conveyance. Food was cooked in the space behind the cottage.'

Years later, Nadira got the opportunity to return Jennifer's hospitality. In 1995, the Prithvi Festival of Contemporary World Theatre had a very difficult time finding sponsors—at the last minute, BPL stepped in but the budget had to be reduced considerably. Nadira and the Ekjute team, recalls Sanjna Kapoor, the festival director, saved Prithvi from 'catastrophe' by offering them the use of an empty apartment for outstation groups, and the entire Ekjute team worked at the festival as volunteers!

Om Katare, who was training at the Filmalaya Acting School, says his group, Yatri, is a Prithvi Theatre creation. Others had come there with a background of theatre, he strayed into theatre after one visit to Prithvi.

'Someone told me about the theatre. Those days we were rehearsing for *Ek Tha Gadha* in Filmalaya Studios. I remember the play I saw at Prithvi Theatre was Avishkar's *Raktabeej* with Sulabha and Arvind Deshpande, and Nitin Sethi.' More than the play, Katare was fascinated by Prithvi's atmosphere. 'I had never seen such intimate theatre. Chhabildas had an informal atmosphere, but here was a fully equipped theatre.

'I sat up in my balcony all night thinking, waiting for daybreak. I had made up my mind to do a play there. At 9 a.m., I landed up at the office—the watchman told me that the manager came in only after 10.30 a.m. So I stood outside Prithvi Theatre

Above left: Ekjute's *Desire Under the Elms* (1982), by Eugene O'Neil starring Nadira Zaheer Babbar, Alok Nath and Ramesh Manchanda. Anupam Kher and Kiron Thakur Singh did this production later, which led to Mahesh Bhatt signing Anupam Kher on for the film *Saaransh.*

Above right: Girija Shankar, Ramesh Manchanda, Ila Arun and Ashok Sharma in Ekjute's *Lower Depths* (1981). This was Nadira Zaheer Babbar's first play performed at Prithvi Theatre.

Right: Sulabha and Arvind Deshpande in Avishkar's *Raktabeej* (1978), written by well-known playwright Shankar Shesh. The Deshpandes were amongst the leading lights of the Chhabildas movement of the seventies, which helped develop experimental theatre in Mumbai.

waiting for Dharamsey Merchant to turn up.
As soon as he did, I told him I wanted to do
a play. He opened his diary and asked,
"When do you want to do it?" It was as
simple as that.'

On 16 January 1979, Katare did his first
play at Prithvi—Santosh Nautiyal's *Ek
Machine Jawani Ki*. After that, he 'gave up
struggling for films' and concentrated on
theatre. It was a long struggle, but he was
determined not to leave theatre. The biggest
support came from Prithvi—Dharamseybhai
in particular. There was no screening
procedure. 'Jennifer and he just wanted
people to come and perform at Prithvi. But
he kept track of the plays, and even if some
substandard comedies did creep in, they

were not given dates later. Soon after this we did *Ek Tha Gadha* and *Kasaibada*.

'Jennifer watched our plays carefully, commented on our work, and encouraged us. That personal touch is important for a group's growth . . . Sanjna has carried forward this tradition. We have done 50 productions, and put up nearly 3000 shows in 24 years at Prithvi Theatre. I even remember the opening dates of all the plays.'

Feroz Khan, who burst onto the theatre scene with Shafi Inamdar in Mahendra Joshi's remarkable production of *Ekshuff* (based on Peter Shaffer's *Equus*), and who was later involved with Jennifer and Kunal Kapoor in managing the theatre, says, 'People were mad about sustaining this activity. One can fault someone's theatre but one can't fault commitment and passion. But for that, there wouldn't have been an audience at Prithvi today. Prithvi provided the foundation on which others were able to continue building.'

Feroz recounts how the entire Kapoor family was involved, every step of the way. There were passionate discussions with the groups all the time, and the actors were involved in the theatre as though it were their own.

Mahendra Joshi's *Khelaiya* (1981), a Gujarati musical based on *The Fantasticks* by Tom Jones and Harvey Schmidt, starring Paresh Rawal, Feroz Khan and Pinty Rao was the first major hit at Prithvi Theatre with a straight 'house full' for its entire run. It was also the first play that ran to a full house on a weekday at 6 p.m., and the first play, as Naushil Mehta remembers, to

Above: Paresh Rawal and Feroz Khan in Avantar's *Khelaiya*, directed by Mahendra Joshi. This Gujarati musical based on the famous musical *The Fantasticks* was Prithvi Theatre's first major 'house full' hit.

Facing page left: Prithvi Theatre's first manager Dharamsey Merchant in his office.

Right: Feroz Khan and Shafi Inamdar in Avantar's *Ekshuff*, based on Peter Shaffer's *Equus*, directed by Mahendra Joshi.

have repeat audiences in phenomenal numbers.

One of Naseeruddin Shah's most treasured memories is dropping by Prithvi Theatre and seeing a crowd of people snaking down the Janki Kutir Lane, right up the main street. 'I wondered what had happened. Was it a fire or something? I discovered they were all standing in queue for tickets for Veenapani Chawla's *Oedipus*, in which I was acting. We were sold out the first day for ten days. It was tremendous—never before in my life had I felt the thrill of that experience.'

Dinesh Thakur's first big hit was *Hai Mera Dil* adapted by Ranbir Singh from Norman Barasch's *Send Me No Flowers*, with more

cooking, her name has got lost in the mist of time!

Sathe's son Baba sat at the box-office for many years and was very popular with the groups. Audiences could depend on his one-line summaries of plays—he was the person credited with coining the term 'social comedy'. Audience tastes had begun veering towards lighter plays, and so they would ask if the play was a comedy before buying tickets. In a stroke of genius, Baba came up with the phrase 'social comedy' for the more serious plays, so that they would not turn away from the counter! Baba suffered from thalassemia, and despite the Kapoors looking after his medical expenses, he passed away at a very young age. His brother Lalit now works with Prithvi Theatre.

Around 1981, Prahlad Kakkar offered to run a café at Prithvi Theatre, on the lines of the Joe Allen chain of theatre restaurants in Broadway and London. The café opened on 18 September, the day *36 Chowringee Lane,* produced by Shashi Kapoor premiered at Mumbai's New Empire Theatre.

Mrs Pinto's homemade breads were a great favourite (her son Neil ran the café for a while after Prahlad gave it up). The café had nice music and the best Irish coffee in town, its rich aroma greeting people as they turned into the narrow unpaved lane that led to the theatre. It became quite the fashion for celebrities to cook and serve at the café, actress Neena Gupta among them.

An amusing incident was reported in the press soon after the café opened. Film star Amjad Khan had been performing in *Chun Chun Karti Aayi Chidiya*—an adaptation of

people crammed into the hall than the permitted 200 and yet more outside begging for tickets. Prithvi Theatre did not even have a 'house full' board at the time. *Hai Mera Dil* went on to become the longest-running Hindi play in Mumbai.

In the beginning Prithvi Theatre did not have a café. Instead there was a small wooden crate with a Primus stove on which Shrawan Sathe, Prithviraj Kapoor's loyal cook, who stayed on to prepare sumptuous meals for the Film-vala's unit across the lane, used to make tea for everyone. A lady used to bring homemade snacks as refreshments for the groups and the audiences. Though Prithvi oldtimers still remember the taste of her

Ken Kesey's *One Flew Over The Cuckoo's Nest*. One night after the performance, Amjad, a tea addict, asked for some tea and was told that there was no milk. It was past midnight, the café was shut and the waiter was perfectly within his rights to refuse the order. The next day, a truck arrived with two buffaloes, with instructions from Amjad that they be tied behind the café so that it would never run out of milk. Of course the animals were returned, and the whole episode dismissed as a joke, but it did make a funny gossip item for a while.

In 1980, artist Tyeb Mehta and his wife Sakina opened a small art gallery in Prithvi's foyer, and a bookshop. These shut down when Tyeb moved to Shantiniketan a few years later, to be revived by Sanjna Kapoor in the '90s.

From Sunday shows, gradually plays began to spill over into weekdays. By 1981, the whole week was booked out. Prithvi Theatre had now become a habit with Mumbai's theatregoers, and a tourist attraction for out-of-towners.

Tom Alter wrote in a newspaper column: 'Strange as it may seem, I always associate darkness with Prithvi Theatre. A darkness which is intimate, and fluid. Coupled with the soft sounds of the sea (now, drowned by the hustle-bustle of traffic and TV sets). Whispers. Performers groping in this dark—fumbling over props. Backstage hands on silent feet. And the song of mind and heart lullabying the hush. Then—the third bell rings (in theatre, it's always three, must be an auspicious number. . .), the houselight dims, the rustling ceases, and there you are,

i.e., all of you, in the wings, ready to make an entry with a thumping heart. And then, in a step, a movement, the first word is spoken, a glance is cast, and the lights blaze away. Gloriously. The darkness—needless to state—recedes with a slight smile, like the tide on the not-so-distant beach. So now, only the play is the thing . . . Yes, this was the first lesson I learnt when I first arrived at Janki Kutir. To a struggler, Prithvi was equal: part dream and part fantasy . . . Since then, plays have come and gone. The festivals are forever etched in the mind's eye. And the darkness which is still there. Peering. At least I've sensed it, whilst performing *Waiting For*

Godot or *Mister Behram,* or *Bloodknot* or *Larins Sahib,* the darkness watched the lights unfold on the play—like a friend. A darkness which watched the grandfathers, the grandmother, the father and mother—just as now, it watches the daughter do her thing!'

Scene IV: Blazing Lights and then Blackout

JENNIFER KAPOOR'S OPTIMISM paid off. After the first few years, with her constant support and the hard work of a few committed groups such as Ank, Yatri, Ekjute, Avantar, Hum and IPTA, Prithvi Theatre registered on the city's consciousness. Stars and strugglers hung out at the café, imbibing Prithvi Theatre's famous Irish coffee and the energy the place exuded. Those were heady days.

Jennifer nurtured Prithvi Theatre like a child. She went there regularly and kept track of everything that went on. Dinesh Thakur remembers seeing her gently stroke the wall—the gesture has been imprinted on his mind. She would sit on the bench outside the theatre and talk to whoever came by. When it was time to leave, she would call out to her faithful Lhasa pup, Yumyum, who always accompanied her, and had the run of the theatre.

Little 'disciplinary' notes to the groups, and duty sheets to the staff would be stuck on the notice board in her clear, slightly untidy hand. 'The stage manager will be present for every performance in the theatre. The programme in the day time will be determined by the particular need of the day, either for supervision or for technical assistance.' Or, 'The theatre manager will have established office hours which will be known to both companies and the public. He will attend a certain number of shows a month.'

Jennifer also wanted Prithvi Theatre to do its own productions, and by 1980-81, she had started inviting directors and actors to take this project forward. That was when Feroz Khan came to be associated with Prithvi Theatre and saw how it functioned from close quarters. 'Prithvi Theatre invested in people, in the regulars ... cancellations were unheard of. The level of commitment it commanded also won over a faithful audience.

'Prithvi had a solution to every problem that a theatre company faced. Prithvi was far more interested in doing a play than in the management, and that was infectious. In many places the management is unconnected with the work that is going on. For them you are almost an encumbrance. With the Kapoors, however, it was a tradition to pay for a performance and watch it no matter how tortuous it was. They realized they were part of a process ... they were not coming to any conclusions about good or bad theatre. They provided great leadership. The place had such vitality that everybody saw a future. It was the only place where a performer had more rights than the management.'

Nadira Zaheer Babbar still gets teary-eyed when she remembers an incident that left a deep impression on her. It happened during a 'house full' show of *Ballabhpur Ki Roopkatha* on a Sunday, just before the 9 p.m. show. Nadira reached Prithvi Theatre a little later than usual and found that one of the actresses had locked the green room from inside. Such a thing was unheard of as it was understood that the space was to be respected. Nadira summoned the stage manager, actor Girija Shankar, and demanded an explanation.

After the first bell rang, the actress in question quietly slunk away. There was a frantic search for her, but she was nowhere to be found. Five minutes before the show, it was impossible to find a replacement. There was just one thing to do, apologize to the audience and cancel the show—which, by the 'show-must-go-on' credo of the theatre, was a shameful thing to do. Nadira was understandably upset and spent a sleepless night.

The next morning, Jennifer asked to meet Nadira. 'I was afraid she would reprimand me for not being able to handle the situation and that my relationship with Prithvi would be ruined,' recalls Nadira. 'But when I got there, she handed me a letter and asked me to read it. It was a letter she wanted to send to all the groups that performed at Prithvi, stating that no group that cast this actress would get dates. I was overwhelmed with relief and gratitude. I was in tears, she hugged me and consoled me . . . I still remember the warmth in her voice.'

By 1983, Jennifer Kapoor realized that it was getting increasingly difficult to run a theatre that was so heavily subsidized. Shashi Kapoor had said of Prithvi Theatre, 'Compare it with any other theatre in the world, it's the cheapest.' Jennifer suggested everyone 'work collectively towards establishing a fund to help subsidize the theatre.'

It is only today, twenty-five years later, that a serious effort is being made to create a corpus fund for the theatre. If the initial years went towards building a corpus of theatre talent, now the focus can turn to the theatre's financial well-being.

Dinesh Thakur thinks that groups like his own, Ank, and IPTA, Majma, Satyadev Dubey's Theatre Unit, Mahendra Joshi's Avantar, Shafi Inamdar's Hum, Nadira Zaheer Babbar's Ekjute, Om Katare's Yatri, Akhil Mishra's Vijeta, Naseeruddin Shah's Motley and others soon started drawing their own kind of audiences to Prithvi Theatre. Some English theatre luminaries like Alyque Padamsee, Hosi Vasunia, Burjor and Ruby Patel, Pearl Padamsee, Nosherwan and Meher Jehangir and Toni Patel also did some memorable plays at Prithvi, though the theatre was primarily meant to encourage Hindi plays.

Above: Director and actor Feroz Khan who was closely associated with Prithvi Theatre and later formed his own group Platform.

Left: Jennifer Kapoor with then Prithvi Theatre manager, Veenapani Chawla at the 1983 Prithvi Festival, the first and only festival Jennifer organized. She passed away on 7 September 1984.

People, who were initially of the view that Hindi theatre was not entertaining, changed their opinion completely after watching comedies like *Hai Mera Dil, Snafu, Ek Tha Gadha* and musicals (*Tathaiya, Khelaiya, Aala Afsar, Saiyan Bhaye Kotwal*) staged by some groups. With time and patience, audiences were trained to accept serious work as well. 'When I saw two sardars crying during a show of *Kamla,* I knew we had arrived,' says Dinesh in jest.

As the theatre's fifth anniversary drew close, Jennifer started thinking of a festival to celebrate the occasion. 'The other reason for the festival,' says Feroz Khan, 'was that the audiences had started following groups. Jennifer was getting worried about groups playing it safe after an initial burst of creativity. She noticed that there was hardly any interaction between groups and their audiences. Every group was finding its identity here.

'The first theatre festival turned that around completely. With it Prithvi Theatre became the yardstick of good theatre.'

Feroz adds, 'The festival had a two-fold motive: economics, and to create excitement on a yearly basis, when Prithvi would bring together the best plays of the year.

'During a festival, groups start to interact with each other and a bonding is inevitable. They watch each other's plays and see the audience's reaction. The 1983 festival was the defining moment of audience growth and also a step towards making Prithvi Theatre self-sustaining. It also marked a peak that the city's Hindi

and English theatre had not scaled in a long while.'

Feroz remembers that Jennifer and he came up with a figure of Rs 50,000 required annually to look after the running expenses of the theatre at that time. One had to look for sponsors. He went around on his bike, slipping applications under the doors of possible sponsors, including liquor and tobacco companies. But there was no response.

It looked as though financial disaster loomed, but help was at hand. B.P. Singh, the chairman of Vazir Sultan Tobacco, and a great fan of Prithviraj Kapoor, Geoffrey Kendal and Shakespeareana, from the good old Gaiety Theatre days in Shimla, had been trying to reach Jennifer. Prithvi's management was unaware of this— Jennifer's phone was dead.

The call came through, however, the day the festival started, and everybody heaved a big sigh of relief.

The first Prithvi Festival was held from 5 to 20 November 1983, with 15 of the best plays that had been performed at Prithvi Theatre till then.

Om Puri recollects Jennifer asking him to stage Majma's hit *Bichchoo* for the festival. 'Ranjit Kapoor who had directed it, couldn't come from Delhi. We did not even have costumes. Jennifer just dragged me to the Film-valas' storeroom, pulled out trunks and let me take costumes from *Junoon*. I couldn't get away. So I organized the show with a new set of actors, and it was a great hit. She came backstage and said, "I told you! You could do it." I admired Jennifer a great deal. She was such an inspiring person, always cheerful and smiling. She never gave the impression that anything was impossible. Such was the spirit of participation that she evoked, that it was difficult to say no to her.'

At the press conference organized to announce the festival, Herbertsons

Right: Vijay Crishna directed a Hosi Vasunia Production—Brian Clarks' *Whose Life is it Anyway?* a play about euthanasia, *w*ith Zarina Mehta, Homi Daruwala and Nikhil Kapoor.

Facing page above: Jayadev Hattangady's Marathi version of Euripides' *Medea*, with his wife Rohini *(centre)*.

Below: Vijaya Mehta's Marathi folk-theatre style production of Girish Karnad's *Hayavadan.* Satyadev Dubey had also done a Hindi version of this play.

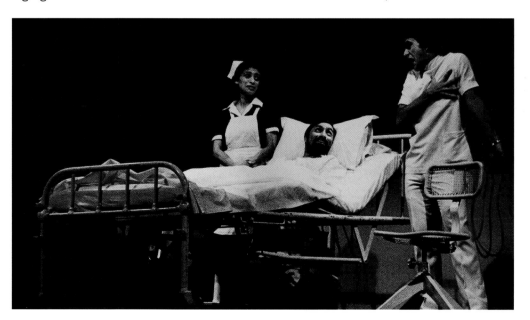

sponsored the cocktails, and an excellent dinner was prepared by Mrs Pinto. Jennifer said that the programme of the festival had been carefully chosen 'to give a varied and balanced variety. Some plays were chosen for popular appeal and some for excellence of production . . . I hope to see various companies working together.'

She also announced plans to construct another building adjacent to the theatre, with rehearsal rooms, a music room, a library and accommodation for visiting companies. 'Obviously,' she said, 'we don't intend to raise this kind of money during the festival, but we hope to make people aware of the need. We want to start a resident Prithvi Theatre Company on a totally professional basis. A 200-seat theatre cannot possibly support such a venture without either state or industry subsidy and we are looking for this.' Over a period of time, some of her hopes of keeping the theatre independent, holding festivals and encouraging new groups, were fulfilled.

The line-up at the 1983 Festival included a British production of *Educating Rita,* Theatre Unit's *Hayavadan,* Ank's *Kamla,* Ekjute's *Chandanpur Ki Champabai,* Avishkar's *Medea,* Shafi Inamdar's *Anjaan Shaher,* Dishantar and Pankaj Kapoor's *Woyzek,* Avantar's *Khelaiya,* Motley's *Waiting for Godot,* IPTA's *Sufaid Kundali, Glass Menagerie* and *Duet for One.* The festival embodied the spirit of Prithvi Theatre, and was probably the high point of Mumbai's English and Hindi theatre at the time.

Soon after the festival got over, groups like Majma and Dishantar disbanded, yet

'And they were all there: the architect who designed the theatre, the manager, the booking clerk, light boys, canteen workers, her personal assistants, and the actors and directors. There, to pay homage to the pioneer of Prithvi Theatre … And as the priests droned on and the flames of incense rose, and filled the air within those charcoal grey walls, I looked up, past the catwalk, where a rocking chair lay dormant up and around the stage left front for there is where she always was at Prithvi, watching closely for the houselights to dim and the performance to commence.'

PEARL PADAMSEE

others split up, while some actors left theatre for good, or at least for a long time.

It was also shortly after the curtain came down on the first Prithvi festival that Jennifer Kapoor took ill. Kunal Kapoor, her elder son, took her to London for treatment. Nobody knew at the time that she would not return.

In May-June 1984, Geoffrey and Laura Kendal came down to Bombay with a production of Aleksei Arbuzov's delightful romantic comedy *Old World.* The play about an eccentric Russian woman and a stuffy doctor is a classic two-hander, and the Kendals were perfect for the parts.

The Kendals had planned to do only a couple of shows at the Prithvi Theatre, but, according to a newspaper report, their old school audiences turned up in hundreds, and they had to cram in as many shows as they could.

The Kendals then toured the country with the play, accompanied by Dharamsey Merchant who did the lights, Rudaba Nanporia (who managed Prithvi Theatre for a while) who handled the music and 15-year-old Sanjna Kapoor, their granddaughter as stage manager. The Kendals were surrounded by fans wherever they went, many of whom had seen their plays as schoolchildren—and had brought their grandchildren to see the play!

Meanwhile, in England, Jennifer's condition worsened. She had been diagnosed with cancer. She wrote to Aparna Sen, 'When actors play the part of a cancer patient, they think they know what it's like . . . but there's really no way of knowing.'

Feroz Khan, who ran the theatre in keeping with her vision while Kunal and Karan were abroad for their mother's treatment, and Sanjna was still a child, remembers that he was in Lusaka, Zambia when he felt a sudden urge to contact Jennifer. So he went to a friend's laundry and booked the call to London.

It took him a while to get through. And when he did, Kunal came on the line and told him, 'She's gone.'

It was 7 September 1984.

In Mumbai, Om Katare's comedy *Unse Mili Nazar* was scheduled to be performed that evening. Kunal called up the theatre with strict instructions not to cancel the show. Katare still remembers, 'She did not want the show to be cancelled. The play was a comedy and we had to perform in such a sad atmosphere. The audience knew . . . nobody was reacting to the play. Some of us broke down afterwards. It was just terrible.'

'I still cannot understand why I wanted to make that call just then,' says Feroz. 'Her death shook me up badly. Kunal and I both returned to India with a sense of responsibility—looking after the theatre. After her, it was a huge burden.'

Soon rumours about closing down the theatre began to do the rounds. A daily even reported that a shoe store would be opening in its place. Shashi Kapoor is reported to have retorted, 'How boring! Why not a bordello?'

Kunal Kapoor says, 'The general perception was that the theatre would just die after Mom. I was adamant that nothing

of the sort was going to happen. We would carry on. We got a lot of support from the groups that were performing in Prithvi at the time, and from the family. Even the press branded Prithvi as a drug den, a prostitution den...'

Such baseless slander was initiated by a handful of vindictive people who had been banned from performing at Prithvi. And nobody from Prithvi Theatre was in any frame of mind to even answer such vicious charges. The family had just flown back to Mumbai where Jennifer was cremated, and headed for Goa with her ashes.

Pearl Padamsee described the condolence meet for Jennifer at Prithvi in a moving tribute: 'And they were all there: the architect who designed the theatre, the manager, the booking clerk, light boys, canteen workers, her personal assistants, and the actors and directors. There, to pay homage to the pioneer of Prithvi Theatre . . . And as the priests droned on and the flames of incense rose, and filled the air within those charcoal grey walls, I looked up, past the catwalk, where a rocking chair lay dormant up and around the stage left front for there is where she always was at Prithvi, watching closely for the houselights to dim and the performance to commence.'

Kunal Kapoor came back to Mumbai and took on the responsibility of running the theatre. 'I had decided we were not going to let Prithvi Theatre fall apart. It was just a challenge. The whole idea behind making it a non-profit trust, was that Prithvi Theatre was not to become a money-making outfit, which eventually the descendants or other

people would squabble over, want to be part of or try to squander away. Mom and Dad wanted to see Prithvi Theatre carry on without stopping. Friends and well-wishers were encouraging, so we got hold of Feroz who was from my generation, and asked him if he would work with us. And he said yes. Then there was Dharamseybhai to help us out.

'The first thing we wanted to do was hold the annual festival even though we were running short of money. Feroz was as attached to the theatre as I was. He, as many others, had a lot of respect for Mom. Dad's friends and other people came forward to help out. We completely revamped the theatre. We renovated it, redid the electricals, installed dimmers that we had got from England, upgraded and painted the hall, and put together this one-month festival . . . as a challenge. She wanted the next one to be a national festival . . . and we did it. This festival too was a success. And then there was no looking back for us.'

The month-long festival in February 1985 brought together stalwarts from Mumbai theatre and the rest of the country under a single roof: Alyque Padamsee staged *Death of a Salesman*; Majma came back with *Uddhwasta Dharmashala*; Veenapani Chawla's Adishakti did a production of *Trojan Women*; Bharat Dabholkar's *It's All Yours Janaab* set him off on a career of Hinglish revues; the Kendals did excerpts from Shakespeare and *Dear Liar*; Habib Tanvir's Naya Theatre came down from Chhatisgarh with *Gaon Ka Naam Sasural, Mor Naam Damad*; Pune's Theatre Academy performed

their classic *Ghashiram Kotwal*, Disha Natya Sanstha from Rajasthan did *Pashu Gayatri*. There were other stellar performances by equally notable groups. Mumbai had never seen such a dazzling array of theatre.

It was quite appropriate to open the festival with Geoffrey and Laura Kendal performing excerpts from Shakespeare, and receiving a standing ovation from the audience. Their performance was preceded by an impressive performance by snake charmers and acrobats outside the theatre, in a spirit of celebration that Jennifer would have loved.

Clare Colvin relates a curious incident from the festival in *The Times:* 'Half an hour before the show of *Ghashiram Kotwal* was due to start, the Theatre Academy's group had still not arrived from Pune. Kunal had an unruffled smile that may have masked a variety of emotions . . . Then, just a few minutes before the curtains went up, the director and leading actor were chatting on the foyer's steps, as if they had all the time in the world, before disappearing backstage to produce one of the finest theatrical entertainments I have seen.'

After the show, the company had dinner on mats spread out on the floor outside the theatre, and everyone sat down cross-legged to eat a Maharashtrian meal served from large buckets into thalis, with their fingers. 'Meanwhile,' writes Colvin, 'the director Jabbar Patel discussed the qualities of Peter Brook's three *Carmen*s at the Bouffes du Nord. It summed up the

Left: At the Memorial Concert for Jennifer Kapoor, Fazal Qureishi with his father, the great tabla maestro Ustad Allah Rakha.

Right: A picture of Jennifer Kapoor is kept in Prithvi Theatre on her birth anniversary on 28 February. On this day, each year, Zakir Hussain performs at Prithvi Theatre. This photograph was taken by Shashi Kapoor at Walsingham School, Mumbai.

Facing page: Eminent tabla player Ustad Zakir Hussain performing at Prithvi Theatre on Jennifer's birthday.

universality of theatre, Jennifer would have loved it.'

The festival went on to become an annual event, which, as Naseeruddin Shah says, 'exposed people to theatre from all over the world and served a function above and beyond the call of duty by giving us an opportunity to see theatre which we would not otherwise. Prithvi gets those plays here. Papaji must be resting content.'

Another tradition was set that year, 1985.

'Mom was a big fan of Ustad Zakir Hussain,' says Kunal. 'She used to enjoy listening to Bismillah Khan, Vilayat Khan and Zakir Hussain. She had always wanted Zakir to perform at Prithvi but that didn't happen while she was around. Zakir finally came to perform at the festival. Since the festival was held towards the end of the month, he performed on February 28, her birthday.'

Ustad Zakir Hussain and santoor maestro Pandit Shivkumar Sharma played together for three hours to a packed house, with people sitting in the aisles, on the stage and even in the wings. At the end of the riveting jugalbandhi, Zakir Hussain said, 'We wish Jennifer a happy birthday and this is our tribute to her.'

Since that day, Zakir Hussain comes to Bombay from whichever part in the world he may be in, and performs every year on February 28 at Prithvi Theatre. The event has gone on to become more elaborate with other performers joining in. The hall and the place outside get packed with people—some come to see a great show, others come to remember Jennifer Kapoor.

A day in the life of Prithvi Theatre.

Sanjna and Kunal Kapoor
at the Prithvi Festival
2003 celebrating 25 years
of Prithvi Theatre.

Act III

Scene 1: After Jennifer

THE THEATRE FESTIVAL and Zakir Hussain became a part of the Prithvi tradition. Twenty years after that fateful day in September 1984, the show goes on—once a day on weekdays, and often three or four shows on weekends. Prithviraj Kapoor was determined that Prithvi Theatres should be, beyond question, a *professional* theatre, rehearsing and staging plays every day, all year round. Shashi, Sanjna and Kunal who continued to live out his dream were no less uncompromising about this. As Sanjna says, 'You can walk into the theatre on any day of the week and watch a play.'

The problems that beset the theatre were as manifold as the doomsayers. Yet Prithvi kept recreating itself. If one group of players disbanded, two sprang up in its place. It was as though the very walls of the theatre inspired people to come forward and do plays. Vijay Tendulkar is quoted as having said, 'Without Prithvi Theatre, Hindi theatre would have no life in Bombay.'

The plays that were staged in the period from the late '70s to the mid '80s had a special character to them. Many who emerged from the happy, creatively invigorating environs of Prithvi Theatre, made lasting reputations. Today, if people like Pankaj Kapoor, Satish Kaushik, Alok Nath, Neena Gupta, Anupam Kher, Shafi Inamdar, Anita Kanwar, Annu Kapoor, are known outside the world of theatre, it is because Prithvi first turned the spotlight on them. Most of them returned to the theatre at some point in their lives. Some sooner than later. Thanks to Prithvi, many had the good fortune to work at this early stage in their careers with directors of the calibre of Satyadev Dubey, Ranjit Kapoor, Mahendra Joshi, M.S. Sathyu and Veenapani Chawla.

Prithvi was doing good work. There was a constant inflow of talent, the café was always buzzing with the excitement of shared experience. As Shafi Inamdar said in an interview, 'Everyone and anyone remotely connected with theatre would hang out there. It had become a fad to be seen at Prithvi.'

But many of the plays staged were far from being mere fads. Twenty-five years later, productions like *Lok Katha 78, Giddh, Poster, Ooljalool, Band Darwaze, Aur Tota Bola, Anjaan Shaher, Aakhri Bisaat, Woyzek, Ek Ruka Hua Faisla, Sufaid Kundali, Desire Under The Elms,* are remembered by

the audience and an instinctive feel for what worked, how to position a play and how to target the right audience. His plays—whether a sex comedy like *Chung Ching* or a family drama like *Ba Retire Thaye Chhe*—had an unabashed commercial quality to them, and he always said he delivered what he promised—there would be no sex in a family drama and no tears in a comedy.

THIS WAS ALSO THE TIME WHEN THE Juhu area and beyond witnessed a real estate boom. The mangroves of Versova filled up rapidly, high rises sprang up like mushrooms, and a new middle class with expense accounts and disposable incomes moved to the suburbs.

In the late '80s, the entry of satellite television into Indian homes proved to be a double-edged sword. For a while, actors and audiences were weaned away from theatre to the idiot box. But there was a positive side to it as well. Many who walked into the auditorium of Prithvi to see a television star perform on stage ended up getting hooked, and came back again and again for the 'live' experience that no soap or sitcom on the small screen could provide. This was how the pioneering groups of Prithvi Theatre succeeded in retaining their audiences.

Today, during a festival of Indian English plays, the story repeats itself. The profile of the audience varies from old faithfuls to hip youngsters who come to see their favourite stars in the flesh—and keep coming back for more.

By 1986, Prithvi Theatre had a new audience, and with that a new set of problems. The ultimate fallout of television and the rise of the middle class was the birth of an audience that demanded entertainment in a quick, easy-to-swallow pill. An audience that did not respect the space, came late and fought to be allowed in, chatted loudly through a show, sat with their feet up, and was, as Feroz Khan put it, 'a monster that had to be got rid of.'

Dinesh Thakur recalls an occasion when a

performers and audiences alike. Groups like IPTA, Samvardhan, Avishkar, Ank, Ekjute and Yatri continue to flourish.

Shafi Inamdar's contemporaries give him a large share of the credit for bringing in a different kind of audience to Prithvi. Because of him, Gujarati audiences came in large numbers. Shafi had a finger on the pulse of

IPTA's production of *Sufaid Kundali* based on Bertolt Brecht's *The Caucasian Chalk Circle*. Shabana Azmi and Sohaila Kapur have a tussle over the child played by Sagar Arya, the son of actress Sulabha Arya.

Facing page: Bhakti Barve and Shafi Inamdar in *Chung Ching.*

bunch of people arrived late for a performance of *Kamla* and raised a ruckus. One of them came on to the stage and sat behind a desk. When Thakur came on, he was astounded to see a man sitting there demanding seats. Thakur had to come out of character and reason with him to go back. On another occasion, he had to interrupt a performance to reprimand an amorous couple who were clearly more interested in each other than in the play!

There were enough groups who still wanted to perform, but a certain desperation crept in; to grab and hold on to fickle audiences, many of the groups were only too ready to lower their standards and pander to the tastes of the ticket-buying majority. The old regulars at Prithvi felt the atmosphere was being polluted.

Looking back now, Feroz Khan, who was in the thick of it with Kunal, says, 'On the one hand, groups started breaking up because they were not ready to reinvent themselves. They were happy to live with the nostalgia of success, because theatre had given them a respectability greater than their talent. And once you start chasing success, you have to do plays of the kind the audiences want, or the economics started catching up with you. Economic reality could not be ignored. People doing popular plays had to understand that these had to be balanced out with serious work, so that the theatre could be economically sustained and at the same time maintain its respectability.'

In 1987, there had been an unpleasant incident—a show of Iqbal Khwaja's *Shakespeare Ki Ramlila* was disrupted by a group of self-styled Hindu activists, and the director himself was attacked and forced to apologize for staging such a play. Prithvi did not believe that censorship was the answer, and did not screen plays before they were staged, yet plays like Shafi Inamdar's *Chung Ching*, Dinesh Thakur's *Bhaagam Bhaag* and Akhil Mishra's *Dum Dum Diga Diga*—all of which had a highly prurient content—came under attack.

Shafi Inamdar had justified his stand by saying, 'I have always wished theatre could be self-sufficient so that one doesn't have to work in a bank . . . I don't want actors who do two shows and then get into films to survive. I want to be able to retain my actors and my audiences so that theatre, whether my own, Dubey's or Naseeruddin Shah's can survive on its own. There is really no point doing shows for five people in the audience and

Prithvi Players' production of the Edward Albee classic, *Who's Afraid of Virginia Woolf* directed by Rajat Kapoor. Kenneth Desai (foreground), with Karla Singh, Sanjna Kapoor and Kenneth Philips.

Facing page: Pearl Padamsee and Sanjna Kapoor in *Gaslight*, directed by Geoffrey Kendal. This was Geoffrey Kendal's last play. He passed away in 1994.

getting good reviews. My stakes in theatre are high and I am not doing it for fun.'

It was a strong defence and there was an undeniable logic in the argument, but finally, Kunal and Feroz had to take a stand in the matter and ban sex comedies as well as excessively 'arty' and self-indulgent productions like Veenapani Chawla's *Savitri*. The decision did not make them popular, but it was the only way to lure the right kind of audience back to Prithvi. Kunal must have reminded himself of his mother's words. In a crack at experimental theatre, Jennifer Kapoor had once said, 'I don't really know what experimental theatre means—if it means *Charley's Aunt* in Kabuki style, that is not what we want.'

It was a tough time for Prithvi's young managers Kunal, Feroz and Rudabah Nanporia. By talking to the groups, reasoning with them, using all their persuasive powers, they were able to work their way through the crisis. But it was a constant struggle to maintain the quality of the plays and keep an eye on the box office at the same time. Kunal recalls, 'Feroz and I would have to decide who to give dates to and why, who to encourage. It was an awful job, and I used to hate it. Twenty-six days in a month, we would get close to 60 applications—how do you decide? To find a balance between maintaining and building an audience as well as pushing the groups, kill the sex comedies and not allow the cheap comedy trash. There was no foolproof answer.'

Perhaps his only consolation was that Jennifer too had often faced the same dilemma. 'I remember Mom would talk about it a lot, and sometimes even get depressed about it. She would be supportive of most of the groups in the theatre, but at home it would get to her.' In the end, the way out of the tunnel was to fall back on the principles by which his parents, and grandfather, had lived. That theatre was a way of life, not a hobby. And that what was unpardonable was a lack of professionalism, honesty and dedication. 'The bottomline was the approach—you were allowed to be a bad actor or director, but not unprofessional. Mom was interested in promoting not just theatre but professional theatre. She had a lack of tolerance or patience for amateurs.'

Following in the footsteps of Jennifer and Shashi Kapoor, Kunal too focussed on making Prithvi a stage that shone a certain kind of light on actors, giving them an advantage, a benefit, that they could not earn out of other platforms like the Tejpal, Bhabha and Sophia auditoria. Whenever an actor responded with a performance that was scintillating, a talent rare or extraordinary, it made the struggle worthwhile. To Prithvi's credit, the days when this happened were not so few and far between.

Feroz and Kunal reintroduced the concept of the 'one-rupee-per-ticket-sold' theatre on weekdays, which brought back the interesting but non-commercial plays by some of the more established groups such as Ank, Yatri, IPTA, Ekjute, Arpana and later, Feroz Khan's own group, Platform. On weekends, they did the popular plays. This subsidy scheme exists even today. Only

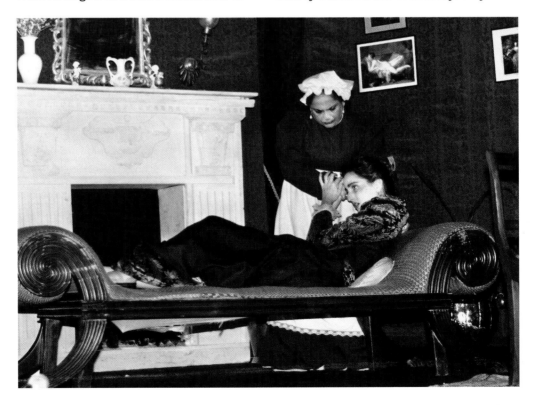

taking inflation into account, the Re1 ticket has become Rs 7.

This rental scheme gave birth to groups like Salim Ghouse's *Phoenix Players*, Iqbal Khwaja's *Hetu*, Makarand Deshpande's *Ansh*, Vikram Kapadia's *Masque* and Zubin Driver's *Spontaneous Assembly,* some of whom have, over a period of time, developed an audience following of their own. In the last few years more groups like Working Title, Out Of Context, Vikalp, QTP and Aranya have come up, so the story continues. So, in their own way, Kunal and Feroz tried not to lose sight of what Prithvi was meant to do and at the same time, keep the economics on track.

What they could not quite succeed in doing was to fulfil Jennifer's dream of a repertory company. In 1992, Prithvi Players, the theatre's own in-house production company, came into being. But it was not a repertory; it was a production company that drew together a group of freelancers for each play. The old warhorse, Geoffrey Kendal, came back to India to perform *Gaslight* for Prithvi Players; Sanjna Kapoor, who had made her acting debut at Prithvi with Janak Torani's *Rashomon* acted in this production with her grandfather from her 'English' side. The talented Rajat Kapoor from the Delhi group, Chingari, directed *Who's Afraid of Virginia Woolf.* The third production was to be a Hindi play directed by the maverick Mahendra Joshi, but his untimely death left a great lacuna on the Mumbai stage.

Before Prithvi Players came into being, Prithvi Theatre had actively supported through logistic and production assistance, the staging of Feroz Khan's first major independent production, Peter Shaffer's *The Royal Hunt of the Sun,* and the Kendals' *Dear Liar.*

But plans for a repertory company never fructified because, as Sanjna puts it, 'Mumbai is just not the right place for a rep, the

Khodus Wadia, Dodo Bhujwala and Nosherwan Jehangir in Feroz Khan's grand production of Peter Shaffer's *The Royal Hunt of the Sun*, which was supported by Prithvi Theatre.

Facing page: Iqbal Khwaja and Vikram Patel in Hetu's *Snafu*, directed by Khwaja.

The problems extended beyond the footlights. Theatre, not business, ran in the Kapoor clan's blood, and Kunal was finding running the café an uphill task. 'It was a nightmare,' he recalls. 'We went through a chain of managers, who would rip us off. It was a tricky business, because Prithvi Café was not just a restaurant—we wanted it to have a character of its own. But at the same time, we wanted everyone to patronize it. It was an ongoing battle to retain the character and ambience.'

A peculiar situation, amusing in retrospect, arose as the café grew in popularity as a watering hole for aspiring actors. Many of them had started getting work in TV serials in the newly commercialized Doordarshan, and soon there was a bunch of gawkers perpetually hanging around the premises, trying to get a glimpse of the 'stars'. Extortionists got a whiff of profit and started bullying the manager of the café for 'hafta' (protection money).

One day, when Kunal happened to be at Prithvi, he was informed that a goonda who had been demanding money was standing outside the theatre. He was a hefty giant of a man, over six feet in height. Kunal walked up to him and said, 'Look here, we don't make money out of this theatre, it is in memory of my grandfather and my mother. To me it is like a temple and I will not tolerate any of this nonsense here. I don't want you to ever come into this theatre again.'

Kunal expected the man to pull a gun on him, or at the very least, land him a couple of punches. Much to his amazement, the

standard of living is too high for a theatre to be able to generate enough of an income to support an individual. And then, the city's more lucrative world of TV and film are a constant attraction for impoverished theatre workers!'

Looking back, Feroz Khan says, 'We had free rein to do what we wanted, but starting a repertory was a different ball game altogether. We couldn't have a repertory without a credible person at the head. Leadership was needed. Jennifer's loss was a loss of leadership. We just kept the tradition going. We didn't add anything . . . it was not possible.'

After the show of Prithvi Players' *Gaslight,* (Left to right) Vijay Crishna, Subash Ashar, Geoffrey Kendal, Sanjna Kapoor, Pooja Ladha and Gerson da Cunha.

Facing page above: Light designer Salim Akhtar with Ila Arun at the Prithvi Café.

Middle: Quasar Thakore Padamsee with his father Alyque and an unidentified person at the Prithvi Café.

Below: Shashi Kapoor dining with some of the actresses from the old Prithvi Theatres Troupe and others: (left to right), Uzra Mumtaz, Kumudini Shanker, Nadira Zaheer Babbar, Sanjna Kapoor, Sarita Joshi, Ranjana Sachdev and Shaukat Azmi.

man said okay and left. He never returned, nor did any of the other goondas, and that was the end of the *'hafta'* hassle.

Reminiscing now, Kunal says that he never thought he would be drawn into looking after Prithvi Theatre. 'Everybody in the family is very independent. We are united but we have our own identities. I was not brought up to believe I would inherit the Prithvi mantle. If I volunteered, it would have to be of my own accord. There was a time when I wanted to be an actor, and (in 1981) I performed in Veenapani Chawla's *Oedipus*, but I was like any other actor in the theatre. In fact, one of the reasons why Mom never performed on the Prithvi stage was because she did not want people to think she had built it to promote herself.'

During *Oedipus*, Kunal had a lot of backstage arguments with director Veenapani Chawla. He hated the concept of evening rehearsals—his condition for acting in plays was that rehearsals should go on all day. In a city like Mumbai, where people had perforce to do day jobs to earn a living, this was unrealistic.

After acting in a few films, like *Utsav, Ahista Ahista* and *Vijeta*, Kunal drifted towards ad filmmaking. For about six years, he kept the Prithvi flag flying with the help of Feroz Khan but with the growing success of his own ad film production company, this became increasingly difficult. So, gradually but firmly, the responsibilities of looking after Prithvi fell in the lap of the 'baby' of the family, Sanjna Kapoor, whose capable leadership took Prithvi Theatre to the next stage.

Scene II: Generation Next

WHEN PRITHVI Theatre was taking shape, Sanjna Kapoor would come with her school friends for picnics at Juhu Beach and play 'chor-police' around the site. She was still a child when the theatre started. Her earliest memories of Prithvi were of falling asleep in the last row, and then, at 15, volunteering at the lowest rung of the ladder, pasting posters all over town, buying decorative diyas, making sure the actors' snacks arrived on time, and acting as an usher at the 1983 festival. Six years later, she recalls walking into the Herbert Bergoff Studios, her drama school in New York, and 'smelling' the festival—it was as

though she had been transported back to her parents' theatre. 'I can't describe the smell, just the memory of that sense of smell,' she says. Perhaps it was the fact that HB Studios was run by the actor couple Herbert Bergoff and Uta Hagen, and their passionate dedication to this small haven of aspiring actors, created the sense of familiarity. She did not know it then, but fate was nudging her towards Prithvi Theatre.

Sanjna spent the year hungrily devouring everything HB Studios had to offer. Acting was what she loved to do, on stage, but the question was, where? The hardcore competitive freelance scenario of British theatre did not attract her. To be part of a travelling repertory was her dream, and this barely existed in the west at the time (it was

in the '90s that repertory theatre revived in the UK). Home was clearly India, but there theatre was still a fledgling and being a professional in this field seemed a dim and distant reality.

Then, as with many dilemmas, fate took a hand, and personal circumstances brought Sanjna back to India after a year. Back home, her acting took a backseat, since, like Kunal, her approach was to be able to rehearse eight hours a day, an impossibility in Mumbai. She kept herself occupied by working with children in theatre, a passion almost as strong as acting for her. At the same time, she found herself inextricably drawn into running Prithvi, as Kunal and Feroz gradually withdrew to other professional commitments. 'I didn't envisage that it would fall so heavily on my shoulders, and I was terrified because it seemed like such a huge responsibility. I knew I had the fire in me. The seeds had been sown by my grandparents, the Kendals, and their stories of their travels in India. It came as a very rude shock to me when I realized that their gypsy life could not be lived any more. But I knew I didn't want to be a freelance actress. I wanted to be part of this lifestyle of a company, and I hoped one day I could make it happen.'

Prithvi's new in-charge started out by watching every play the theatre staged. She was horrified by most of them—'by the plays and by the degradation of the audience'. What distressed her most was the fact that very few groups were staging plays designed for the space that Prithvi provided. 'In fact they would bring box sets which were horrific. They should have stuck to a proscenium stage if that's what they were looking for. You look at these actors who are into "fast-food acting" and think that they should not be on stage. Even the audiences were beginning to react to the plays as if they were watching TV. They would talk to each other while the play was on, as though they were in their own drawing rooms!'

There is a point in the growth curve of any organization when it must entertain new ideas, explore new avenues. For Prithvi, it was a question of the right people coming together at the right time. As Sanjna took over the reins of the theatre,

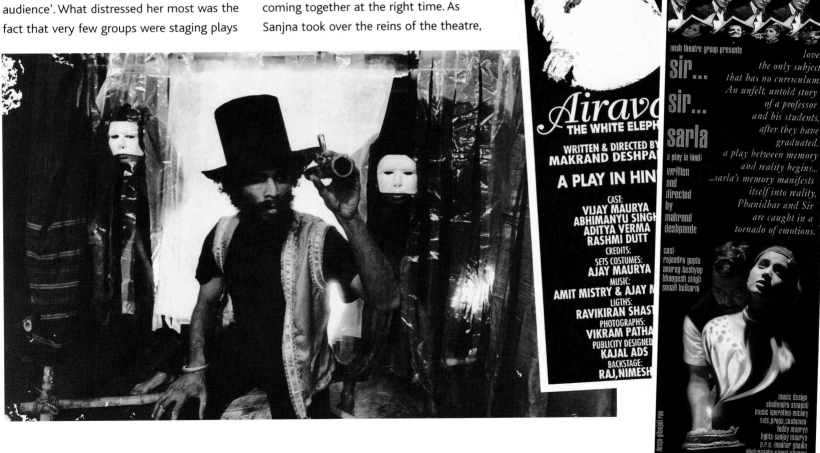

Directed by RAJAT
KAPOOR with Atul,
Vinay, Joy, Rajat & Sheeba
At Shri Ram Centre, main
auditorium 18th, 19th, 20th
& 21st November, 7:00 p.m.
Book your tickets in
advance at the music shop,
khan market, fact and
fiction, vasant vihar the
shop, regal building &
www.delhitickets.com [for
home delivery]

with ideas of her own on how to run it, a new breed of young directors, playwrights and actors was coming in too, with an agenda quite different from that of the earlier generation.

Makarand Deshpande, Vikram Kapadia, Ramu Ramanathan, Rajat Kapoor, Atul Kumar, Janak Toprani, were all relatively new in theatre, and though they did not have an emotional attachment with Prithvi as some of the earlier groups did, they were sincere and dynamic. They got it all ready-made—an ideal venue, well-laid tracks of modern Hindi theatre that had been developed over a decade, an audience habituated to Prithvi and a young person at the helm who was willing to encourage them. The fact that they are all still around over a decade later, proves that Sanjna did provide the leadership and vision Prithvi required. She deftly balanced the old with the new so that audiences got a dose of the familiar along with the fresh.

Sanjna's earliest influence was the late Mahendra Joshi, whose untimely death in 1993 was a great blow to experimental Hindi and Gujarati theatre. ' He had stopped doing theatre for a while, and his group, Avantar, was taking a break,' she recalls, 'but he was amazing for me. He lived miles away in Dahisar, but he would meet me at 10 a.m. at the Prithvi café, and help me work out the nitty-gritty of the children's workshops that I wanted to start. Even though there was no payback for him, he helped me put the economics of it all in perspective. I loved his madness—he would walk for 45 minutes till he found a cab which had the music he wanted to hear—he would not get into any other cab! He was a delight to work with.'

One of Prithvi's greatest charms was that people had the ability to just walk in through the door and share their dream, and find a way of making it happen. The lighting expert Kaiwan Mistry, who passed away in 2000 was one such person. Recalls Sanjna, 'Kaiwan just walked in one day and offered his services. After many years of technical frustration, finally there was someone who would breathe life into the staff. He helped to rewire the entire lighting system and offered to come in and take care of things. He loved what he was doing and he educated me about what lights were.'

Makarand Deshpande, whom Sanjna credits with being her only sounding board in the years of loneliness she felt while reviving Prithvi, turned out to be the most prolific and imaginative of the younger lot of theatre people, and the most committed to the medium. 'Makarand, like Mahendra Joshi, works with a vigour that many of our theatre workers lack,' says Sanjna. 'They make their team work till they sweat . . . people like Mak were an inspiration because of the madness with which they think. The 1995 Platform Performances came alive because of him.'

Like Om Katare did 15 years earlier, Makarand calls himself a product of Prithvi. To date he has written, directed and produced 25 full-length and 30 platform plays—a record output. 'When I first entered Prithvi Theatre, I said where is the theatre? For me it was like the extension of a classroom or rehearsal space. I loved the

sound of my voice here. Prithvi gave me a
solid grounding in theatre. I used to enjoy
writing, performing and just being here for
long hours. I enjoyed the informal
atmosphere where I could do anything. If
there was regimentation, I wouldn't work
here. We could come and rehearse at 7 a.m.
or midnight. No other theatre allows that.'

A platform play (performed outside the
theatre before the main show) for the '92
festival was the result of his first attempt at
writing. The following year, he wrote *Dream
Man*, a full-length play. Before long, he was
staging a fresh play every two months—
something that Sanjna, who would have
preferred the plays to have longer runs, was
not entirely happy with. 'But if I didn't do so
many plays, I felt I was not utilizing the
space. Prithvi made me write plays—and a
play is not a play till it is staged.'

Makarand had a wild and vivid
imagination, and also an impatience with his
own work which often made him start
rehearsing a play before it was finished, and
keep adding to it while the shows were on,
so one performance of a play could be very
different from the next. People often
complained that they could not understand
his plays, but enjoyed them nonetheless. It
took him many years to make his work
accessible, and also let a play run long
enough for it to 'grow'. More often than not,
before one play could settle down, Makarand
was ready with his next.

An idiosyncrasy of writer-director Ramu
Ramanathan was his penchant for writing
letters to the director after he had seen a
play. The criticism was often constructive:

what he wrote about *Who's Afraid of Virginia Woolf* was discussed among the cast. 'The anti-naturalism of "the thing" was dramaturgically very exciting and communicative,' said the letter, handwritten on lined paper. 'However, in absence of an All-Important Technique for classification—it was clearly evident that each of your four actors descended from four different acting schools—there is the danger of signification being everything. And so, although I personally freaked on the intuitiveness of gesturing which transcended the sameness of the plot . . . there was the risk . . . that these physical ordering mechanisms, appeared more real than the characters on which they were composed. To a large extent, this might be the reason why (as an audience), I was left with a disconnected lump of experience and not the coherence of a whole . . . '

Then, in 1996, Ramu came up with the idea of holding a 3-day festival of Indian English plays. In 1997 Theatre Positive was born, and in its quiet, small, unpretentious way, made a serious contribution to theatre. Theatre Positive readings were held on the first Monday of every month. Writers came up with original plays, which they 'tested' out at these readings, and some of them went on to become significant full-scale productions.

BY THE '90S, THE PROFILE OF THE audience as well as the actors had altered again. A play like *Tumhari Amrita*, in which the two actors, Shabana Azmi and Farouque Shaikh sat on stage and read letters, became an unprecedented success. Adapted by Javed Siddiqui from AR Gurney's *Love Letters* and directed by Feroz Khan, the play could well have been designed for the intimate Prithvi space. Audiences seeking their weekend entertainment now co-existed with a crowd of college students and young professionals, who appreciated the offbeat plays of Makarand Deshpande (*Kasturi, Sir Sir Sarla*), Rajat Kapoor (*C For Clown*), Atul Kumar (*The Blue Mug*), and Quasar Thakore Padamsee (*A View From the Stage*). The shift in the character of Prithvi's audience prompted Naseeruddin Shah to remark that while the older crowd had stopped reading after college level Shakespeare and Shaw, the younger generation was very well informed.

Around this time, the media also started taking more interest in the cultural life of the city, and theatre folk who had hitherto been neglected, started acquiring celebrity status. In 1978, the opening of Prithvi Theatre had warranted a small paragraph on the inside pages. Now camera crews started turning up in full force to cover the festivals and other events—especially if there were film or TV stars participating.

Sanjna prided herself on being good at 'creating atmosphere'—and Prithvi now combined the homely warmth the older groups had been so attached to with a behind-the-scenes professionalism that made it possible for her team to organize major festivals without a hitch. And the festivals mixed the formal with the flamboyant in an inviting package.

A quarter of a century after the curtains first rose at Prithvi Theatre, the old guard—

Satyadev Dubey, Naseeruddin Shah, Dinesh Thakur, Nadira Zaheer Babbar, Om Katare, K.K. Raina and of course IPTA—continue to grace the floorboards, as do Lillete Dubey, Mahabanoo Mody Kotwal, Rahul da Cunha, Vikram Kapadia, Ramu Ramanathan and Quasar Thakore Padamsee, whose plays in English have their own following at Prithvi amongst the young crowd.

For a while after the first bunch of NSD graduates and other theatre actors had

Lillete Dubey, Neha Dubey and Shernaz Patel in Primetime's *Breathe In Breathe Out*, directed by Dubey and adapted from Edward Albee's *Three Tall Women*.

Facing page: Boman Irani, Firdausi Jussawala, Shernaz Patel and Veera Abadan in Rage's *Six Degrees of Separation* directed by Rahul da Cunha.

been absorbed into television and films, Prithvi had stopped being the haunt of aspiring actors. But now, thanks to the extensive media coverage it has become fashionable to do theatre and be picked up by talent scouts. Today, Prithvi Café is once again abuzz with anticipation and aspiration.

A quality that Sanjna has clearly inherited from her mother Jennifer, is the ability to lead a team. She delegates responsibility to her associates, yet retains a certain degree of control even when her twin responsibilities as a wife and mother take her away to Delhi for long periods of time. Though she does express dismay at the fact that the theatre is not full every day, she also appreciates what Prithvi has been able to achieve over the years.

'Prithvi had actually spoilt groups and actors. For instance, they stopped using their voices well. My biggest frustration today is that there just seems to be an all round laziness. But, in spite of it all, in the last 4-5 years there have been happy moments, there have been sparks of something interesting happening, people are trying different things. The magic of theatre is because it's live and tangible and in front of you. It needs to surprise you, in a quiet gentle way.'

Prithvi Theatre made sure the stock of surprises never ran out.

And the show goes on . . .

Scene III: Spreading Wings

Tobacco company, who sponsored the very first Prithvi Festival in 1983 and then continued to support its annual deficit and festivals for ten years—a unique and hugely beneficial association.

But in 1992, VST changed its policy towards support of the arts, and focussed instead on sport—which left Prithvi in the lurch. That year, Goldflake stepped in to sponsor the festival. Thereafter, Prithvi had no annual sponsor for a period of four years. These were tough years, when the theatre literally survived hand-to-mouth. Various members of the family subsidized the losses with their earnings from films.

Ironically, this was the time when Sanjna took over the reins of Prithvi with full force. She acknowledged the truth that neither she nor her family were any good at 'selling' Prithvi (it took years of experience and failure to develop into the charming fund-raiser Merchant describes her as!) and so they should simply continue doing what they were good at—creating ideas and events that would propagate the development of theatre. So, at a time when finances were at their lowest, and each month was a struggle, Prithvi's activities kept increasing. Events that became part of Mumbai's cultural calendar all took birth during this period—the children's theatre workshops, Prithvi Players as well as Little Prithvi Players which produced plays for children, Theatre Positive, Platform Performances on weekends outside the theatre, the annual Keli Festival of traditional

ISMAIL MERCHANT ONCE SAID OF Sanjna Kapoor, 'She is a great charmer. Even if she asks you for money, you cannot refuse her because the asking is accompanied by great style...a sense of seduction.'

Money, rather the lack of it, was a spectre that loomed large over Prithvi right from its earliest days. 'It's crazy,' Sanjna once said in an interview. 'Nobody will believe the way Prithvi is run. People literally work for us for free. It runs on goodwill, and we have just about minimal staff. Because the festivals get hyped people think we are loaded, but we're not!'

Prithvi Theatre was built by private donations and no government funding. It managed to survive thus for five years. It was in its fifth year that the theatre managed to get its first sponsorship from the Vazir Sultan

performances from Kerala, supporting groups like Rangvardhan with their festivals. The Prithvi Gallery was revived, the annual Prithvi Festival grew bigger, and children's theatre festivals were organized.

Each of these events had its own sponsorship, ranging from CEAT, Frooti and Hong Kong Bank, to BPL and a host of others. Finally, in 1997, the persistence and hard work paid off, and Maxtouch got in touch with Sanjna to look at sponsorship opportunities. Thus began an association with what is today known as Orange, the cellphone giant.

The idea was to get the finance needed for the theatre to survive without selling its soul, and the marriage has proved to be a compatible one. The Orange lanterns and buntings add to the charm of the place, they do not scream 'buy' and at last, even though the theatre is not quite flush with funds, it is not in a perpetual state of deprivation. The association has given Orange the unique opportunity to be associated with one of the country's oldest and finest cultural houses, while giving Prithvi the benefit of long-term financial support which has breathed life into several new projects—among them, the creation of a monthly newsletter, *PT Notes* (edited by Ramu Ramanathan), and monthly shows at Horniman Circle Gardens, an open air public performing space which created a new venue and broadened the theatre's audience base.

Despite the pressures of running a tight ship, over the years, Sanjna has been able to turn Prithvi into a complete cultural hub, rather than just a venue for plays. 'That's

Carmen Funebre by the Polish company Teatr Biuro Podrozy. The performance on stilts during the Prithvi Festival 1998, was a protest against war.

Facing page: Ratan Thiyam's Chorus Repertory Theatre, from Manipur, performing *Uttarpriyadarshi* at the 1997 Theatre of India Festival.

what is different about Prithvi,' she says. 'We are not just an auditorium for hire, and I think the family has always had a very serious approach to what we wish to achieve.'

The Prithvi Art Gallery was reopened in November 1994, after ten years, with an exhibition of Laxman Shrestha's works. Thereafter, the opening of a new exhibition on the first Sunday of every alternate month, with cozy informal brunches under the bamboo awning, along with live music, has become an event to look forward to. Music, art and a great brunch—these are the ingredients that typify the Prithvi brand of informality and seriousness.

Above (left to right): Audiences watching a Platform Performance at the Theatre of India Festival in 1997; Shashi Kapoor, Shafi Inamdar at the Prithvi Festival 1993; Satyadev Dubey, A.K. Hangal, Sandip Das (COO of Orange) and Shashi Kapoor at a Prithvi Festival inauguration; The IPTA Theatre Festival dedicated to world peace and nuclear disarmament, at Prithvi Theatre.

In the eight years that followed, until 2002, the gallery hosted more than 50 exhibitions with an eclectic mix of young and upcoming as well as established artists, such as Badri Narayan, Lalita Lajmi, Altaf, Navjot, Deepak Shinde, Bhupen Khakkar, Jin Sook, Samir Mondal and Anjana Mehra. Presently, it is undergoing something of a sabbatical, with plans to reopen in 2005 with an exciting new aim.

In the words of Feroz Khan, 'Sanjna gave Prithvi a personality—she dedicated herself to it, and her integrity as a person gave it value. The festivals she started doing, the new areas she opened up,

gave it a reputation as a place of significance.'

In 1995, Sanjna managed her first major festival without Feroz Khan's assistance. Called Contemporary World Theatre, the festival brought to Delhi and Mumbai international theatre performances unique in their respective forms.

The 1996 festival, Theatre of India, created an even bigger stir as the plays were staged in multiple venues across Mumbai, and on account of the quantity and quality of plays. 'Since then,' says Sanjna, 'our festivals with partners across the country, be it in Pune, Bhopal, Goa, Trivandrum or

Below (left to right): Vrindavan Dandavate, Akash Khurana, Shashi Kapoor, an unidentified guest, Shafi Inamdar, Deepa Gahlot, and Ila Arun at the 1989 Prithvi Festival; audience watching a platform performance including Sanjna drinking the famous Irish coffee; people at the café; Om Katare and Shishir Sharma at the Postcards from Mumbai Festival in 2002; a Platform Performance outside the theatre during the Prithvi Festival, 2000.

Bangalore, helped propagate our effort in bringing the very best of international theatre to India. The almost "bombardment" of festivals, whether it is the annual Prithvi Festival, or the Footsbarn Travelling Theatre from Europe, whom we have presented thrice in Mumbai from 1995 till 1999, or the partnership with Keli, or international puppetry festivals—through the sheer magnitude and regularity of these events, is how, I think, Prithvi has managed to create such a following today, such a charged atmosphere at each performance.'

Over the years, Prithvi has become a favourite of the media, as more 'stars' and

celebrities get involved. Whereas in the early days the theatre suffered from a lack of attention, now perhaps it suffers from a glut. Sanjna agrees that 'there can be a negative side to the media hype—to oversell something leads to misplaced expectations. Prithvi has felt this in the recent past. 'An event which actually needs to thrive off its immediate community and survive from a more organic, subtle form of communication, is actually our greatest challenge today—to connect to our community and make ourselves be of value to it. Even though the gloss and tamasha of media hype is at its highest today, the saddening thing is that almost all channels of media communication choose to ignore the necessity to review art and theatre.

These pages have been systematically deleted from newspapers across the country. They are all too busy "selling" to have any space to critique and analyse the arts and their role in society today. Again, a challenge for us to find this space of communication, critique and analysis.'

SANJNA'S OWN PERSONAL PASSION was for children's theatre. When she took over the management of Prithvi and was appalled by the audiences, she decided to work with children, so that they could learn to appreciate theatre at a young age. In 1990, Summertime at Prithvi came into being, and in 1992, Little Prithvi Players was born.

Puppetry
Painting
Arts and Craft
Children's plays
Acting
Mask Making

Enroll at Prithvi
Theatre & Y.B.
Chavan, Hurry!
Limited entries

Summer
time
at Prithvi

Modelling
Cartoons
Mime

ril 15th to
e 10th 2001

ty of 27 creative
re workshops
en

years

urch Rd., Mumbai 400 049. Tel.: 614 3046
Near Mantralaya, Mumbai 400021 Tel.: 2045440

She found enthusiastic support in people like Ramnath Tharwal, Anita Salim, Meena Naik, Vidya Patwardhan, Neeraj Kabi, who enjoyed working with children. At the workshops, children learn everything from acting, story-telling, dance, mask-making and puppetry, to classical theatre, Shakespeare, the epics and Kathakali. It is Sanjna's belief that this exposure opens a window and when they watch a play, they can understand and appreciate it. Hopefully, when they are older, they will form an ideal audience. 'Fourteen years later, we are already tasting the fruit of our seeds!' she says.

One of the rules that Sanjna lays down for her workshop conductors is to stay away from TV, films and ad jingles 'which surround children like the plague'. She believes children have to be given other associations. Another strict rule is that no names are given out to people, so that children are not brought to the workshops in the hope of being spotted by a talent scout. These restrictions notwithstanding, the workshops have grown steadily in popularity from that first summer. Now each May, there is a rush for registration, and on an average, each workshop has around 30 students. Sanjna recalls that even those children who were dragged in reluctantly by their parents, have become permanent fixtures today.

Children participating in Summer Workshops that Prithvi Theatre organizes every year, since 1991. Sanjna Kapoor, Ramnath Tharwal, Anita Salim, Neeraj Kabi, Atul Kumar, Loveleen Mishra, Asif Basra, Vidya Patwardhan and Divya Bhatia have conducted these workshops. Speech, drama, mask-making, pottery, art and craft, story-telling are some of the activities covered at the workshops.

Some of Little Prithvi Players' productions have achieved a fair degree of popularity, the landmark, of course, being Ramu Ramanathan's *The Boy Who Stopped Smiling*, a Grips play which travelled all over the country, did a hundred shows in just two years and is still going strong. The Grips style of theatre was created over 30 years ago in Berlin, in response to the moralistic pantomimes that existed for children, and, through speaking in the child's language, aimed at opening up discussion with children and adults on issues that were 'taboo'—like fear of hospitals, racism, bullying, etc. The plays typically have a lot of music in the rock/pop style, and have adults playing all the parts, including those of the children, done with such finesse that you forget they are adults. This allows for a certain professionalism and longevity of the production. It was Dr Mohan Agashe who introduced Grips to India, and Ramu

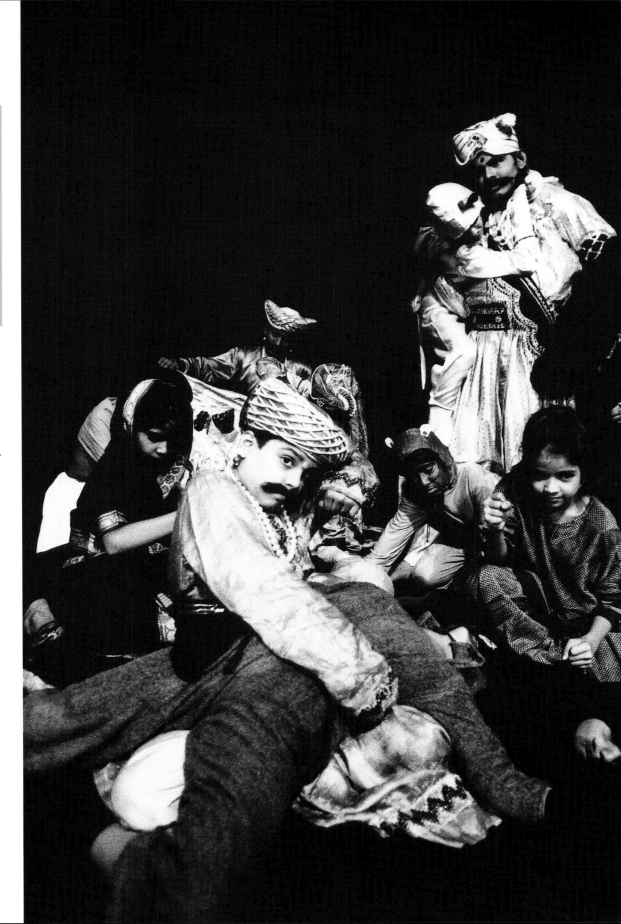

Ramanathan wrote *The Boy Who Stopped Smiling* after attending a workshop organized by him.

Directors like Om Katare and Nadira Zaheer Babbar were inspired to do children's plays after seeing the success of the summer workshops, and if imitation be the best form of flattery, the best acknowledgement has been the copycat workshops that have sprung up all over the city.

IT WAS IN SANJNA'S TIME THAT PRITHVI Theatre literally grew wings and moved out of the confines of its own premises, to other venues in Mumbai and even outside the city. In 1996 Sanjna and her team 'adopted' Horniman Circle Garden, a public park in South Mumbai, immaculately kept by the Tata Trust, and turned it into a vibrant cultural space. To this day, the pick of Prithvi productions are performed there on weekends, opening up a unique experience to a new audience. The CEO of a company sits next to a street urchin who has peeked in out of curiosity, or next to a eunuch as

South Africa's Ellis and Beki's *Skadonk*, and Footsbarn Travelling Theatre's *The Winter's Tale*, performed during the Prithvi Festival at South Mumbai's Horniman Circle Garden. Since 1996, on the first weekend of every month, Prithvi Theatre presents plays in the open air at this enchanting public garden. The performances are free and open to all.

Sanjna discovered once much to her delight, and enjoys a play. 'Spaces get human credibility. New audiences are created, this is not just theatre for theatre people,' she says.

The most significant area of growth, change and involvement has been the annual Prithvi Festivals. Sanjna was a 15-year-old volunteer at the first festival in 1983. Later she assisted Feroz in managing the festivals, the most successful being the theme-based Playwright at the Centre.

'Another reason for holding these theme-based festivals is to check if there is an audience for a certain kind of theatre. Do people want to see what we hold so dear to our hearts? Surprisingly we have always found an audience which justifies the need for a theme. I believe that if one is doing something with which one has a personal attachment, in whatever field of expression, there will always be someone who will understand the sentiment.'

Feroz Khan, who had been a co-director of the festival along with Kunal, for many years, feels that it is as much a celebration as a stock-taking exercise. 'The idea,' he says, 'is to involve as many people as possible, performers as well as audiences, and to use the festival as an audience pull, to get new audiences.'

Theatre director, actor and enthusiast Divya Bhatia, who volunteered for the 1989 festival and stayed on as co-director, believes that after the first few years, the festival stopped being just a 'Prithvi thing' and became a Mumbai event, 'and an exciting doorway into the world of theatre, that was a shot in the arm to practitioners of theatre'.

Not just that, it exposed audiences to a wide spectrum of theatre experiences, from the youthful energy of platform performances outside the theatre, to groups from abroad to Grips theatre and puppetry. Now festival plays have repeats at other venues in the city, with one festival travelling to Delhi, another to Pune.

According to Sanjna, Divya not only took on the 'donkey work' that a festival entails—'piles of letters, faxes, files. It is rewarding to have people like Divya bring in their time, energy and vision. Or someone like Atul Kumar, who organized the festival in Delhi in 1995; he is so methodical and organized that I learnt a lot from him.'

Were it not for the Prithvi initiative, Mumbai audiences might never have seen plays by Indian groups from other parts of

the country, nor would they have had the chance to see some fine international work. For the latter, Sanjna was criticized. Certain regular theatre groups in Mumbai boycotted the international performances, saying that they would never have the financial or technical facilities available in the west, so what was the point of watching theatre from there! The 'poverty-stricken' Indian theatre could never match up to western theatre—a poverty of the mind, was Sanjna's furious response. Her answer to them came in the form of the milestone Postcards from Bombay Festival in 1999, at which local groups were invited to perform new plays. If Prithvi stood for quality, it needed to generate that quality. Such a dazzling array of local theatre had not been seen in Mumbai in a long time. Plays like *Sakubai, Sangeet Debuchya Muli,* and *Shobhayatra* broke new ground. Ironically, after years of theatre producers bemoaning the lacuna in Indian theatre writing, three-fourths of this festival threw up original Indian playwrights!

In 2002 there was a repeat of this theme, with Sanjna demanding premiere shows, and again the city's theatre folk were galvanized into action to come up with superior plays like *Black With Equal, Mahadevbhai* and *Haravlele Pratibimb.*

The following year, there was another festival of national theatre, with plays handpicked by Prithvi's team who had travelled all over the country and selected the best work. In a show of solidarity that is needed if theatre has to grow, 50 delegates from different states met to

discuss and debate the community of theatre. A few new venues were added and the festival made accessible to the whole city. That a festival of this scale was put together by a small team seems like a miracle.

'The scale, reach, impact have undergone massive refurbishment,' says Divya. 'The Prithvi festivals break boundaries of venues, locations. So many volunteers stay back year after year. Given the amount of work, effort and money that go into a festival, unless it is a celebration for many people, we are not satisfied. The real aim is to connect with an audience. 'The reasons for doing the Prithvi Festival have evolved. The Prithvi Festival is a brand by itself connected to theatre—it gets more publicity and hype than Prithvi Theatre. Along with developing audiences, the festival also becomes a vehicle for introspection.'

Over the years, the annual event has become as much a part of the city's cultural consciousness as Prithvi Theatre itself.

Scene IV: Into the Future

SATYADEV DUBEY SAID about Prithvi Theatres, 'It is the greatest thing in Bombay in the last 50 years. After a long time, I've found actors coming out feeling happy, feeling that they have established some rapport with the audience. It could have been a stillborn child, but it's alive, it's kicking.'

A quarter of a century later, the same could be said about Prithvi Theatre. That is an achievement in which the inheritors of Prithviraj's legacy can justifiably take pride.

But when a space has turned into an institution, without which it is impossible to envision a city's cultural landscape, it is inevitably time for some 'what-now' soul-searching.

Twenty-five years ago, Prithvi Theatre was a pioneer in an open field, now other auditoria fill the city's skyline—some more expensive, others less welcoming or encouraging of non-commercial theatre—but venues to explore nonetheless.

So where does Prithvi go from here? Sanjna puts it thus, 'In 25 years we have achieved a lot. We have generated enough work, and there have been shifts and changes. What Prithvi can do now is push the limits of everybody's quality.'

This is easier said than done in an environment where audiences have other entertainment options and look upon theatre as just another evening out to enjoy. Audiences are willing to spend huge sums of money to see even bad plays starring film and TV stars. In an ironic twist to the tale, theatre, that was all along seen as a stepping-stone to showbiz, now confers status and respect on those who have achieved fame and fortune on the silver screen.

For Sanjna, a constant concern is to 'avoid forcing a culture on the audience. I dread becoming the dinosaur of a cultural institute, which is dead from within, but keeps itself alive only by way of flashy events. I want to be associated with theatre which is needed and socially relevant. And from this feeling stems my occasional dejection. I question myself about the activities of Prithvi.'

Sunil Shanbag takes the outsider's perspective: 'Prithvi theatre has got caught between being a theatre for hire and being a theatre that sets trends. If you want to set trends then do it all year round. Today you can count on the fingers of one hand the groups that work consistently and do reasonably good work. Prithvi has to be proactive, seek good work or create a parallel system without pitching it against regular groups. Create new time slots. If the theatre thinks a play is good, go out of the way, support it. Choose a handful of plays and support them. Pick plays that fit into the Prithvi spirit. Prithvi needs to have a sharper profile.'

Feroz Khan, who once faced the flak with Kunal when they took the decision to ban sex comedies, feels the time has come for Prithvi to once again take a strong stand, and define more clearly the kind of theatre it wants, while at the same time understanding the compulsions of the groups. 'They have to state what they want so there is a vision that everybody is able to understand. They need to take on, say four or six productions a year, run these plays for three to four weeks, promote them well, make sure the returns are there, so they can say, these are the plays we want happening at Prithvi. A vision statement for the next two to three years is very important. Invest in ideas, in people. In the end the building is nothing, it's what happens inside.'

'Six productions a year! A producer's nightmare!' exclaims Sanjna. 'If I had my way, I would decide on every play, the director and the cast and then let them grow. But there are two questions which we

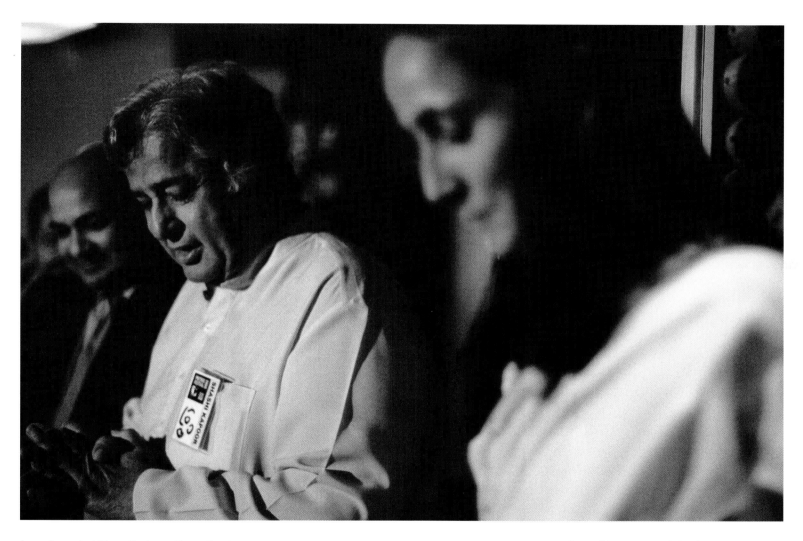

have been battling all along. Does theatre really matter? If Prithvi closed down tomorrow, would it make an iota of difference to anyone in Bombay?

'With that question there has to be a huge entrepreneurial effort to reach out to whom it matters. If the circus disappeared from our lives, it would be a loss. To me a circus is pure entertainment, but also pushing a human being's limits, that fabulous taking away of the breath by some

Sandip Das (COO of Orange), Shashi Kapoor and Sanjna Kapoor at the inauguration of the Prithvi Festival in 2000.

amazing achievement of the human body . . . the magic of it. So we have to question the relevance of what we are doing, whether we are required, needed, effectual at all, and then make a really serious effort to make that difference. And I don't think that's happening enough.

'What does happen is these hugely amateur efforts in pockets across the country, where people do ten shows of one play and close down and think they have achieved something. Ten shows? It's nothing, it's meaningless! If you do a production and put that effort into it, you have to be able to sustain your activity. So you need to have a certain professional attitude to what you do. You have to hook into the community and the community should think that you are important ... whether it is working with schoolchildren or college children or going into a puja sabha ... '

Sanjna defines a good play as one that provokes thought, gives a new perspective, something that 'lingers with me for days—that is the greatest thing.' But she has the grace to admit that many of the plays performed at Prithvi today fall short of these criteria, and that the theatre needs to look outwards and draw inspiration from what others are doing in other parts of the country.

At the same time, she admits, that Prithvi has to strengthen its own infrastructure. 'One is getting more and more focussed now but there is a lot we have to sort out in our own working system.' One of the biggest stumbling blocks is that Prithvi still does not have a corpus of funds to give it an independent financial base. 'It makes us very vulnerable because we are completely dependent on sponsorships. We've been very lucky with sponsors but we need to revisit and redefine our approach to sponsorship and our survival, and we are building a corpus now. There are times when I feel deeply lonely, desperate to find like-minded people with like-minded vision. The fact that one grew up in an atmosphere where theatre was taken as a profession makes one even more critical of what we see around us.'

Ramu Ramanthan's initiative had given birth to Theatre Positive, Satyadev Dubey ran Monday workshops for years and also came up with the idea of informal, unstructured do-your-own-thing evenings, out of which the popular *Dhamal* emerged in 2002. This was an experiment that took place on the first Monday of every month, when an open platform of 10-minute performances was created on the Prithvi stage, curated by a *sutradhar* (narrator). The idea was to encourage the emergence of a wide range of forms of theatrical expression, as also to encourage people to literally 'take the stage' with their ideas.

> When Zohra Segal had asked Prithviraj why he had named his company Prithvi Theatres, in the plural, he had replied that it was his dream to have a theatre in every town in India.

Today, Sanjna's effort is to pull in people who are concerned 'with the bigger picture' and also willing to be part of the unglamorous side that involves actually managing the theatre, making it run. 'The bigger vision is always to try to promote theatre and to see good theatre,' says Sanjna

She meets with the groups at least a couple of times a year, and when she is in Mumbai, her office is open to all. Now that she is spending more and more time in Delhi with her 'new' family, new channels of communication have to be forged. Makarand

Deshpande suggests regular interactions between old and new groups, but Sanjna feels that the groups should take this initiative themselves and not wait for Prithvi to serve everything up on a platter. This is taking place slowly but surely—at times, events serve as the catalyst, such as Rage Productions' Writers' Bloc festival of nine plays in early 2004, which were written at the Royal Court Workshop where veterans like Om Katare and Rahul da Cunha shared a platform with youngsters like Nitin Batra and Apoorva Kale. With more young people entering the scene, both as performers, viewers and organizers, Prithvi seems to have become the new bastion of Indian English theatre, without consciously moving in that direction. Having been created essentially to support Hindi theatre, today there is an equal amount of English theatre at Prithvi, with bits of Marathi and Gujarati as well. It is a theatre family that is spreading, individuals with no umbilical connection to Prithvi Theatre but all of whom are fired by theatre.

'Quantity we have achieved, we need to look for quality...even if it means a few dark nights. I have a feeling something exciting will happen in the next five years.' says Sanjna.

ACCORDING TO A NEWSPAPER REPORT ON the opening night of Prithvi on 5 November 1978, 'The trustees of Shri Prithviraj Memorial Trust under whose aegis the workshop had been constructed, hope that the space they have built will be stimulating and challenging both to the directors and actors who use it, as well as exciting and involving for the audience.'

But was this indeed all that Prithviraj Kapoor's dream envisioned, or did he have a larger canvas in mind? When Zohra Segal had asked Prithviraj why he had named his company Prithvi Theatres, in the plural, he had replied that it was his dream to have a theatre in every town in India. Jennifer Kapoor had come closest to picking up on that dream. She had once said in an interview, 'What we hope the existence of Prithvi Theatre will encourage or create is a lively professional theatre. We wish more such theatres would be built all over the country with similar aims so that productions designed for Prithvi Theatre could play elsewhere.'

The biggest tribute to Prithviraj Kapoor's memory would be a chain of Prithvi Theatres run by individuals as committed as the members of the Kapoor family. At least one Prithvi-inspired theatre Ranga Shankara is being built by Arundhati Nag in Bangalore. As Nag herself puts it, 'Twenty-five years after Prithvi Theatre, another mad person has come up.' Sanjna says, 'She has created a baby that will never leave home and will need constant mothering. More than funds, it needs human resources, people who can think, dream and see things through to the end.' And Sanjna hopes that theatre will go from strength to strength.

Meri zindagi ek musalsal safar hain
Manzil pe pahunchoon to manzil bada de.

(My life is an unending journey,
Were I to reach my destination,
may it recede forever.)

—Prithviraj Kapoor

A green room in
Prithvi Theatre.

GODREJ-GE
APPLIANCES
presents

FOOTSBARN
THEATRE'S

The Winter's Ta
By William Shakespeare

...un 19th, 8 pm, Horniman C...

...IN COLLABORATION WITH...   TAJ PRESIDENT

PRITHVI
FESTIVAL

NANDIKAR'S
SHESH
SAKSHATKAAR
IN BENGALI
DIRECTOR : RUDRAPRASAD
SENGUPTA
MAIN CAST : RUDRAPRASAD
SENGUPTA
GAUTAM HALDER

...00 P.M.
TKTS: Rs. 10

TUE 7

NANDIKAR'S
ANTIGONE
IN BENGALI
DIRECTOR : RUDRAPRASAD
SENGUPTA
MAIN CAST : SWATILEKHA
SENGUPTA
RUDRAPRASAD
SENGUPTA

9:00 P.M.
TKTS: Rs. 10

WED 8

ARPANA'S
KISSE
IN HINDI
WRITER : SHAFA...
DIRECTOR : SUNIL...
MAIN CAST : UTKARS...
APARAJI...

9:00 P.M.
TKTS: Rs. 10

...ACTORS ON
...ACTING
...WORKSHOP

10:00 A.M. — 5:00 P.M.

MON 13

NAYA THEATRE'S
AGRA BAZAAR
IN URDU
WRITTEN AND DIRECTED BY
HABIB TANVIR

6:00 P.M. & 9:30 P.M.
TKTS: Rs. 10

TUE 14

NAYA THEATRE'S
CHARANDAS
CHOR
IN HINDI
WRITTEN AND DIRECTED BY
HABIB TANVIR

6:00 P.M. & 9:30 P.M.
TKTS: Rs. 10

CRITICS...

No 127

मुखबिरवाला

जब च...
बन...

One Penny
Two Penny
Directed by: Sanjna Kapoor

CREATIVE
KIDZ
Presents

Little Prithvi Players
Three One Act Plays
For
Children

And English Play

SILVER
JUBILEE
SHOW

SUNDAY
2ND JAN 11 AM
SOPHIA

Rs. 60/-

Seat..........

Rights of Admission Reserved, No Refund.

...king Space in Side the Compound.

Rang Vidushak's
Vatan Ka Raga',
Horniman circle garden

...27 dec'98 7:30 pm

Max Touch
PRITHVI
children's festival '98

LAEZER'S
CHILDR...
LESSER...
IN ENGLISH
WRITER : MARK...
DIRECTOR : PEARL...
MAIN CAST : FARID...
RONNI...

6:00 P.M. & 9:30 P.M.
TKTS: Rs. 50

24

PRITHVI THEATRE
1945-1996
भारत INDIA 2.00

PRITHVI
FESTIVAL
2000

in association with

orange

SETTING
THE STAGE

JUHU HOTEL

SOUTH
AFRICAN
AIRWAYS

PRITHVI
FESTIVAL

198...

...TION WITH
...
Industr...
Limited

NANDIKAR'S
ANTIGONE
(BENGALI)
8th NOV...

Prithvi Theatre

...Y WARNING: CIGAR...

Time :

THE PRITHVIWALLAHS AND PRITHVI EVENTS

1922-26

Prithviraj Kapoor gave his first stage performances at Edwards College, Peshawar.

1928

A young Prithviraj Kapoor arrived in Bombay to join films.

1931

Prithviraj Kapoor joined Grant Anderson Theatrical Company.

1944

Prithviraj Kapoor inaugurated his professional travelling theatre company, Prithvi Theatres with *Shakuntala*. Raj Kapoor designed the sets, sound, lights, music and costumes. Shammi Kapoor performed as Bharat. Shashi Kapoor played an extra.

1947

At 13, Jennifer Kendal gave her first major stage performance—Viola in Shakespeareana's *Twelfth Night*, and came to India with Geoffrey and Laura Kendal.

1953

Shashi Kapoor joined Prithvi Theatres and toured with them for 5 years.

1957

Shashi Kapoor joined Shakespeareana, toured with them for 2 years, and performed in over 16 plays.

1958

Shashi Kapoor married Jennifer Kendal who then joined Prithvi Theatres.

1960

Prithviraj Kapoor closed down Prithvi Theatres after 2662 shows across India, over 16 years.

1972

Prithviraj Kapoor passed away.

1975

Shashi Kapoor created Shri Prithviraj Kapoor Memorial Trust in the memory of Prithviraj Kapoor. Both Shashi and Jennifer Kapoor became trustees.

1976

Shashi Kapoor established Film-valas, his film production company which produced 6 films in all.

MEMORABLE PRODUCTIONS
1978-2004

Akhri Shama: This play is Kaifi Azmi's poignant account of the last *mushaira* in Delhi as the city desperately clings on to the remnants of its culture under threat from the British. Bharat Kapoor played Ghalib in revivals of this play while other IPTA stalwarts formed the rest of the cast of poets at the mushaira.

All The Best: Devendra Prem's Marathi play *All The Best* was already a huge success when Feroz Khan decided to produce its Hindi version. Three friends, one blind, the other deaf and the third mute—all fall in love with the same girl! They need each other to communicate with her, and the comedy borders on the hysterical as each one tries to elbow out the other to win over the girl.

Andha Yug: Satyadev Dubey revived this Dharamvir Bharti masterpiece many times over. In the play which retells the Mahabharat from the Kauravas' point of view, Naseeruddin Shah's portrayal of Ashwatthama was simply brilliant. The cast had the likes of Amrish Puri, Akash Khurana, Mohan Bhandari and Sunila Pradhan.

Aur Tota Bola: Satyadev Dubey directed the Hindi version of Chandrashekhar Kambhar's Kannada play, done in a folk style, reworking a myth about fertility to include an anti-feudal statement. Sunila Pradhan, Sunil Shanbag, Utkarsh Majumdar and others were part of the cast.

Ballabhpur Ki Roopkatha: Ravi Baswani directed this Badal Sircar comedy about an impoverished prince trying to sell his haunted mansion. Eventually, when he finds a buyer, more skeletons come out of the creaking cupboards.

Bambai Ke Kauwe: Shafaat Khan may not be a very prolific playwright, but all his works have left a mark on Mumbai's theatre scene. *Bambai Ke Kauwe*, directed by Ganesh Yadav, originally in Marathi, was a dark, socio-political satire about two Mumbai social workers in cyclone-ravaged Gujarat, faced with a peculiar demand—procuring crows necessary for Hindu funeral rites.

Begum Jaan: Written by Javed Siddiqui, Nadira Zaheer Babbar's play about an old singer, played by Nadira herself, still living in her dream world of royal suitors and magnificent *mehfils*, has a quaint old world charm about it. The canny old woman, however, tries to trap a journalist who wants to write her biography, into marrying her daughter (Juhi Babbar), so that she can escape her crumbling world.

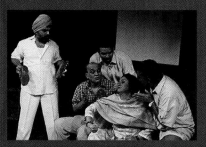

Black With Equal: One of the best original contemporary plays in English, Vikram Kapadia's *Black With Equal* is set in an ordinary Mumbai housing society. A general body meeting triggers off a crisis and buried communal feelings are raked up once again as the satire moves towards an overstated, though plausible, climax.

Chanakya: A trendsetter on the Gujarati stage in the early nineties, *Chanakya* written by Mihir Bhuta and directed by Dinkar Jani, was enthusiastically received by audiences. Manoj Joshi played Chanakya, the master strategist, and continued to do the role for over a decade.

Children of a Lesser God: Pearl Padamsee directed this intense Mark Medoff play about a deaf-mute woman and her stormy but tender relationship with her teacher, with Farida Peddar and Ronnie Screwvala in the lead roles.

Chun Chun Karti Aiee Chidiya: After he became a star, Amjad Khan appeared in this powerful adaptation of the Milos Forman film *One Flew Over the Cuckoo's Nest*. He plays the man sent to a mental asylum where he finds that sane people are infinitely more dangerous than the so-called lunatics. The play was directed by Amjad Khan's brother Imitaz Khan. Meenal Patel played the cruel nurse who persecutes the hero.

Class of 84: Rahul da Cunha's *Class of 84* is about a bittersweet walk down memory lane. Seven friends meet after 17 years at the beach home belonging to one of them to mourn the death of their common pal Jojo. Over a long and emotionally unsettling evening, secrets are spilt and regrets aired. Da Cunha got together some of the finest stage actors like Rajit Kapoor, Sohrab Ardeshir, Rituraj, Radhika da Cunha, Joy Sengupta and Zafar Karachiwala, in this play.

Cyclewala: Sunil Shanbag directed this intriguing Vijay Tendulkar play about an over-protected man's fantasy journey on a bicycle and the strange people he encounters. Utkarsh Majumdar and Astad Deboo acted in this play.

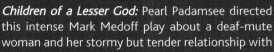

1977

Shashi Kapoor realized Prithviraj Kapoor's dream—Prithvi Theatre.
Kunal Kapoor joined The Birmingham Repertory Theatre School as an actor.

1978

Prithvi Theatre was inaugurated on 5 November.
Feroz Khan gave his first performance at Prithvi Theatre in *Ekshuff* directed by Mahendra Joshi.
Sanjna Kapoor, Shashi and Jennifer Kapoor's daughter, gave her first performance, with grandparents Geoffrey and Laura Kendal.
IPTA: The Indian People's Theatre Association was established in 1943 during the upheavals of the Bengal famine and World War II in order to reach out to the common man. Stalwarts of literature, performing arts and theatre were part of IPTA—Shambhu Mitra, Kaifi Azmi, K. A. Abbas, Balraj Sahni, Salil Choudhury, Chetan Anand and the current bearers of the torch—A.K. Hangal, M.S. Sathyu, Ramesh Talwar, Anjan Shrivastava, Javed Siddiqui, Kuldeep Singh, Salim Arif.
Theatre Unit/Samvardhan: Satyadev Dubey has been single-handedly upholding the banner of Hindi theatre in Mumbai for over 40 years. From Dharamvir Bharti's *Andha Yug* (1962) to the recently staged *An Actor Dies But*, Dubey has directed over a hundred plays with his groups Theatre Unit, and later with Samvardhan and other groups like Aawishkar and Arpana. Some of his memorable productions include *Aur Tota Bola, Aadhe Adhure, Ooljalool, Sambhog Se Sanyas Tak, Raste*.
Theatre Group: Alyque Padamsee first produced and directed *Killers* with Theatre Group (1946). His major productions were *Hamlet, A Streetcar Named Desire, Kabaret, Jesus Christ Superstar, Evita*. But his other works like *Tara, Final Solutions* and *Roshni* were performed at Prithvi Theatre.
Avishkar Theatre Group: Avishkar Theatre Group heralded the experimental theatre movement in Mumbai over 40 years ago. After the era of Vijay Tendulkar, Arvind and Sulabha Deshpande, Satyadev Dubey, Jayadev and Rohini Hattangady, Arun Kakde has been getting young talent like Chetan Datar into its fold.
Majma: Om Puri was the moving force behind Majma, which he founded with his NSD and FTII friends—Naseeruddin Shah, Karan Razdan, Satish Shah, Neelam Mansingh Chowdhary, Rohini Hattangady, Ratna Pathak Shah and others. After doing *Uddhwasta Dharmashala, Bichchoo* and *Ek Ruka Hua Faisla*, the group folded up after 5 years.
Ank: Dinesh Thakur has devoted himself completely to theatre. Ank has done a variety of plays from the works of Mohan Rakesh, Vijay Tendulkar, Girish Karnad to Molière and Neil Simon. *Tughlaq, Kanyadaan, Anji, Jaat Na Pucho Sadhu Ki, Khamosh Adalat Jaari Hai, Hamesha, Baki Itihaas, Beewiyon Ka Madarsa, Aazar Ka Khwab, Jis Lahore Nahin Dekhya* are some of Ank's popular plays.

Yatri: Om Katare leads one of the most prolific Hindi theatre groups in Mumbai—over 50 productions and 5000 shows. Some popular Yatri productions include *Ek Tha Gadha, Kasaibada, Kaalchakra, Dhoondte Reh Jaoge, Dilli Ooncha Sunti Hai* and *Chor Chor.*

Vijeta: Akhil Mishra started his stage career with Yatri, then started his own group Vijeta along with his wife Manju Mishra. The group did plays like *Wah Re Peerghulam, Jaal, Tim Tim, Miss Julie* and *Sach.*

Hum: Shafi Inamdar was one of the most successful theatre producers, directors and actors on the Mumbai stage. His plays like *Neela Kamra, Ada, Shabana II, Ba Retire Thay Chhe, Reshamgaanth were* major successes. His wife Bhakti Barve was also an acclaimed stage actress.

Ekjute: Under the leadership of Nadira Zaheer Babbar, Ekjute had seen many NSD and FTII alumni pass through its portals—Sushmita Mukherjee, Ravi Baswani, Kiron Kher, Anupam Kher, Anita Kanwar, Rajendra Gupta, Ashish Vidyarthi. *Lower Depths, Yahudi Ki Ladki, Jasma Odhan, Ballabhpur Ki Roopkatha, Sandhya Chhaya, Court Martial, Baat Laat Ki Halaat Ki, Sakubai, Dayashankar Ki Diary, Begum Jaan* are some of Ekjute's memorable plays.

Avantar: The genius of Mahendra Joshi and the playwriting inputs from Chandrakant Shah helped Avantar produce some great plays like *Tathaiya, Khelaiya, Ekshuff.* Joshi's premature death cut short a very promising career.

Motley: Naseeruddin Shah, Tom Alter and Benjamin Gilani, all from FTII, established Motley and devoted themselves to doing plays that excited them. The group's *Waiting for Godot* has been a great favourite. Shah's *Court Martial, Julius Caesar, Androcles and Lion, Manto Ismat Haazir Hain* and *The Prophet,* have all been highly appreciated. Shah's wife Ratna (with whom he did *Dear Liar,* directed by Satyadev Dubey), daughter Heeba and son Imaad are also part of the Motley family.

PRITHVI CAFÉ: An intrinsic part of creating atmosphere . . . the open-air Prithvi Café under the bamboo, with Irish Coffee, brownies, endless cups of tea, samosas, food . . . all lend themselves to the FULL theatre experience!

Adishakti Theatre Company: Veenapani Chawla's Adishakti Theatre Company was founded in 1981. She has trained in theatre, Chhau, Kalaripayattu, Koodiattam, Kathakali and Dhrupad—and brings eclectic influences into her work—*Oedipus, A Greater Dawn (Savitri), Impressions of Bhima, Brhanalla* and *Ganapati.* Adishakti has found a home in Pondicherry.

Vikalp: The group comprised the Avantar 'gang' started in 1981, but didn't get active till Naushil Mehta returned from the US. Mehta produced a revival of *Pokhaar, Hriday Tripti;* and more recently directed *Patra Mitro* and one segment of *Tran Gujarati.*

Doongaji House: Toni Patel picked up Cyrus Mistry's award-winning play that had been languishing for want of a daring producer, and turned it into a moving portrayal of a Parsi family. Hormusji (Nosherwan Jehangir) and Piroja (Meher Jehangir) live in genteel poverty in their crumbling flat, with memories of better days. The play had some memorable characters, superb performances, and acute observations about life in Mumbai. Chetan Datar later did a Marathi version of this play.

Ek Akeli Ek Subah: Sushmita Mukherjee did a tremendous job with her one-woman shows based on the plays by Dario Fo and Franca Rame. Adapted by Atul Tiwari, the two short plays were 'serious' comedies about the exploitation of women. The first play portrayed the dreary life of a woman who gets up early in the morning to do household chores while her husband snores in bed, then she goes out to tackle an exhausting assembly line job. The second play was a scary and pathetic account of a woman locked up in the house by her husband when he goes to work. Saira Essa from South Africa performed this play at the 1987 Prithvi Festival.

Ek Aur Dronacharya: Shankar Shesh's play, directed by Subhash Dangayach, is about the loss of idealism in the modern age, aptly portrayed by Arvind, a college professor, who can never live up to his own principles and constantly bows down to the powers that be. Arvind's situation is compared to that of Mahabharat's Dronacharya, who had been compelled to demand Eklavya's thumb in sacrifice to protect the interests of his royal wards.

Extremities: William Mastosimone's play *Extremities,* directed by Raell Padamsee, was a disturbing portrayal of the politics of rape. When a woman (Pervin Dastur), attacked by a man (Shivkumar Subrahmanyam) puts up a fight and eventually succeeds in thwarting the rape attempt and tying up the man, she is faced with a deluge of sexist prejudice.

Final Solutions: Alyque Padamsee directed Mahesh Dattani's *Final Solutions,* a scathing comment on communal prejudices as a Muslim man takes shelter in a Hindu household to escape from a mob. Dattani won the Sahitya Akademi Award for this play.

Ganapati: This play with music, percussion, and rhythms, performed in English, interpreted the various stories about the birth of Lord Ganesh. Director Veenapani Chawla explored the various social, physiological and spiritual dimensions of creation and creativity in this play. Myth and legend were treated by Chawla in other productions as well including *Impressions of Bhima* and *Brhanalla.*

Going Solo 1 & 2: Three directors—Anahita Oberoi, Vikram Kapadia and Rahul da Cunha—collaborated on *Going Solo,* a series of monologues on various aspects of womanhood. The experiment was such a success that the team came up with *Going Solo-2* with a theme, 'Living on the Edge', made up of 12 monologues performed by actors like Seema Biswas, Zafar Karachiwala, Sohrab Ardeshir, Darshan Jariwala, Anahita Oberoi, Divya Jagdale, Lovleen Mishra and Radhika da Cunha.

Kasturi: Arguably Makarand Deshpande's most accomplished play, it took up the topic of female sexuality and built a web of surreal relationships involving two women and a man. Ratna Pathak Shah, Mona Ambegaonkar and Sudhir Pande emoted their roles to perfection. Arundhati Subramaniam translated the play into English, and *Musk Maiden* was directed by Vikram Kapadia.

Khamosh Adalat Jaari Hai: Dinesh Thakur's version of the Vijay Tendulkar play *Shantata Court Chaalu Aahe!* is about some actors who, conduct a mock trial to kill time. In course of their improvisation they are confronted with a number of realities about women in India.

Idgaah: When IPTA started Balmanch, it did *Idgaah*, a production for children with child actors such as Rajeshwari Sachdev, Sagar Arya and Shaily Sathyu. The play, directed by Madhu Malti was based on Munshi Premchand's story about a poor boy Hamid, who was gifted some money by his elders on Id. Instead of purchasing sweets for himself with it, he buys a *chimta* (tongs) for his grandmother, so that her hands do not get burnt when she makes rotis.

Ismat Aapa Ke Naam: Naseeruddin Shah, Ratna Pathak Shah and Heeba Shah brought out the humour, pathos and anger of Ismat Chugtai's stories through their portrayal of three of her famous stories. Naseeruddin Shah picked up the *'kahani ka rangmanch'* tradition, that converts short fiction into theatrical pieces and gave it his own unique touch. Later he returned to Ismat with his equally fine production *Manto Ismat Haazir Hain*, then to classic fiction with *Katha Collage.*

It's All Yours Janaab: Bharat Dabholkar did an Indian English version of P.L. Deshpande's Marathi comedy *Tuza Aahe Tuze Pashi*, and started the trend of 'Hinglish Revues' like *Bottoms Up* and *Monkey Business.* Harish Patel, Atmaram Bhende and Manmohan Krishna acted in this production.

English theatre scene of the eighties, doing plays like *Nuts*, *The Subject Was Roses*, *Shabana II* (with Shafi Inamdar's *Hum*).

Hosi Vasunia Productions: A very good actor himself, Hosi Vasunia has been a dynamic producer of English plays—*Whose Life is It Anyway?*, *Agnes of God*, *Steel Magnolias*, *Barefoot in the Park*, *A Funny Thing Called Love* and *Rummy Game*.

Ace Productions: Raell Padamsee, daughter of Alyque and Pearl Padamsee, did her first play *Interpreters* with Sabira Merchant and her mother. She then set up Ace Productions. Her plays include *Family Ties*, *Act of Faith*, *Games People Play*, *Laughing Wild* and *Let's Talk Honey*.

Stage 2: Toni Patel did not direct too many plays, but the ones she did were highly appreciated—*Mister Behram* and *Doongaji House*, both original Indian scripts in English.

Rage: Rahul da Cunha along with Shernaz Patel, Rajit Kapur and wife, Radhika da Cunha, have to their credit successful productions like *Love Letters*, *Larins Sahib*, *I'm Not Bajirao*, *Jesus Christ Superstar*, *Going Solo 1 & 2*, *Class of 84* and *Pune Highway*. Rage presented the Writers Bloc Festival of original Indian plays.

1985

MEMORIAL CONCERT: Held since 1985 on Jennifer Kapoor's birthday. Designed and conducted by Ustad Zakir Hussain, this unique annual event of music in the excellent acoustics and atmosphere of Prithvi Theatre brings alive the *baithak* experience for our audiences.

1987

Kunal Kapoor established Ad-Filmvalas, his ad film production company.

Masque: Vikram Kapadia has more than 18 years of theatre experience as director, actor and writer. His directorial ventures include *Six Characters In Search Of An Author*, *The Dining Room*, *Master Harold And The Boys*, *Romeo and Juliet*, *Musk Maiden* and *Black With Equal*.

1988-89

Shashi Kapoor established the Trust as a Research Foundation.

1989

Sanjna Kapoor joined Herbert Berghoff Studio, New York.

Zero Theatre: Actor, director, playwright Shiv Subrahmanyam began with a production of *Blood Knot*. In recent times he has done acclaimed original plays like *Snapshots From An Album* and *Irani Café*. Shiv is married to talented actress Divya Jagdale.

1990

Sanjna Kapoor started working with Kunal Kapoor and Feroz Khan at Prithvi Theatre.

Jameelabai Kalali: K.K. Raina directed Ila Arun's adaptation of Mario Vargas Llosa's *La Chunga*. The play was set in a remote Rajasthani outpost where Jameelabai (Ila Arun) runs a seedy bar. The disappearance of a girl after a night of drunken gambling by a group of men, raises a lot of questions.

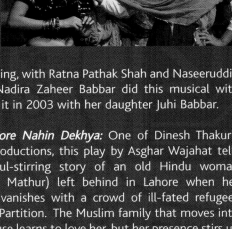

Jasma Odan: Shanta Gandhi's Bhavai-style folk musical about a young married woman coveted by a king, about teaching the king the value of honest labour, was colourful, earthy and entertaining, with Ratna Pathak Shah and Naseeruddin Shah putting up brilliant performances. Later Nadira Zaheer Babbar did this musical with Sushmita Mukherjee in the title role, and revived it in 2003 with her daughter Juhi Babbar.

Jis Lahore Nahin Dekhya: One of Dinesh Thakur's best productions, this play by Asghar Wajahat tells the soul-stirring story of an old Hindu woman (Preeta Mathur) left behind in Lahore when her family vanishes with a crowd of ill-fated refugees during Partition. The Muslim family that moves into her house learns to love her, but her presence stirs up a communal problem.

Mahadevbhai (1892-1942): Mahadev Desai was Mahatma Gandhi's secretary from 1917 till his death in 1942. Desai maintained extensive records of Gandhi's conversations and letters in his diaries. The eight-volume diaries are the source for Ramu Ramanathan's excellent play on Gandhi's life and times as seen by his faithful companion. Jaimini Pathak was outstanding in the play.

Mahatma vs Gandhi: Feroz Khan's English play based on a Gujarati novel captures the troubled relationship between Gandhi and his rebellious elder son Harilal. The cast of the play underwent several changes. Naseeruddin Shah, Boman Irani and Seema Biswas have all been part of it. *Mahatma vs Gandhi* has also been performed in Marathi and Gujarati.

Main Zinda Hoon: Nadira Zaheer Babbar adapted John Osborne's 1956 classic *Look Back in Anger*, first with Anupam Kher, then Suneel Sinha playing the Indian Jimmy Porter, Vicky, who rebels against religion, society, his wife (Sohaila Kapoor/Seema Kapoor), and his friend (Darpan Mishra).

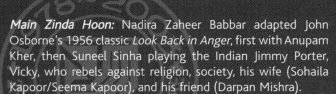

Master Phoolmani: Based on Satish Alekar's *Begum Barve*, this Manoj Shah play in Gujarati, starring Utkarsh Majumdar and Chirag Vora, goes back to the Bhangwadi tradition to tell the tragic tale of an actor who dreams of living as a woman and even bearing a child. His dreams clash with the harsh reality of his life as a man and an actor past his prime.

Merchant of Venice: Salim Ghouse did a cheeky and colourful version of Shakeaspeare's play with actors dressed in bright clothes with mime make-up, on an almost bare stage. Ghouse played Shylock, his wife Anita Salim played Portia and Uday Chandra, Antonio, who manages to save his pound of flesh.

Mister Behram: Gieve Patel's moving play, directed by his wife Toni Patel is about power struggles in a Parsi family. Mister Behram (Nosherwan Jehangir) adopts a tribal boy (Rajit Kapoor), becomes obsessed with him, and slides inevitably towards tragedy. Tom Alter, Shernaz Patel and Havovi Kolsawala also acted in the play.

Mojila Manilal: Bhupen Khakkar's tongue-in-cheek but scathing satire on middle-class morality was ably directed by Mahendra Joshi. Set in a Mumbai *chawl*, it deals with the changes in the loves of two middle-class couples when Manilal (Javed Khan) seduces the bored housewives by buying them *gajras* and flirting with them in English. The zany comedy had a memorable set design by Kakkar.

Nuts: Rahul da Cunha made his directorial debut with this Tom Topor play produced by Burjor Patel. The story of a high-class call girl who kills a customer in self-defence, but refuses her parents' attempts to have her declared mentally challenged to avoid a scandal, had a high-powered cast— Shernaz Patel, Ruby Patel, Rajit Kapoor, Homi Daruwala, Nosherwan Jehangir, Ratan Batliwala and others.

Pratibimb: Mahesh Elkunchwar's bizarrely funny play about a man who loses his reflection was brilliantly directed by Sunil Shanbag in its Hindi version. Satyadev Dubey did the play in Marathi. For the 2002 Prithvi Festival, Chetan Datar did a theatrical-dance version, *Haravlele Pratibimb*, with Rajashree Shirke and Vaibhav Arekar.

Romeo And Juliet: Vikram Kapadia took a crack at Shakespeare very early in his career, and did a very imaginative and energetic *Romeo and Juliet*, which attracted a young audience, and established Kapadia as a director to watch out for. And he did not disappoint.

1991

Primetime Theatre Company: Lillete Dubey set u[p] the company with Mahesh Dattani's *Dance Like [A] Man*—her most successful production. Dubey's othe[r] productions include *Muggy Nights in Mumbai, 30 Day[s] in September, Siren City, Breathe in Breathe Out, Womanl[y] Voices* and *Zen Katha*.

Spontaneous Assembly: Playwright director Zubi[n] Driver and actor Kenneth Philips began with plays lik[e] *Worm, Room Full of Rain, Two Sets of Fou[r] Monologues, One For The Road*, amongst others, befor[e] closing down because Philips moved to Germany. I[n] 2004 Zubin Driver started a new theatre group calle[d] The Open Theatre.

SUMMER WORKSHOPS AT PRITHVI: Held annuall[y] for young people aged 6 to 16, these workshops aim t[o] develop a future audience and unleash the creativity i[n] youth through theatre and creative arts workshop[s] conducted by professionals, at venues across Mumba[i]. Participants get to see children's plays free for a year a[t] the Prithvi Theatre.

1991-92

PRITHVI PLAYERS: Prithvi Theatre's in-hous[e] production company was launched with Patric[k] Hamilton's *Gaslight* directed by Geoffrey Kendal. Th[e] second production, Edward Albee's *Who's Afraid o[f] Virginia Woolf* was directed by Rajat Kapoor. Both thes[e] productions performed extensively in Mumbai and o[n] tour nationally. A third production in Hindi, to b[e] directed by Mahendra Joshi, was planned but n[o] realized due to his untimely demise.

1992

LITTLE PRITHVI PLAYERS: The company produce[s] one-act and full-length plays for young people—som[e] with young actors, some with adult actors—in Hind[i] and English, and performs across Mumbai and Indi[a]. Tom Stoppard inaugurated the Prithvi Festival– Playwright at the Centre and gave a public lecture.

Reactions: Ganesh Yadav and Kishore Kadam, bot[h] fine actors have done plays like *Angan Tedha, Bambai K[a] Kauwe, Kaal*, and *Mera Kuchh Samaan*.

Poor Box Productions: Mahabanoo Mody Kotwal an[d] son Kaizad have done plays like *Once I was Young Now [I] am Wonderful, (W)hole in the Head, Shirley Valentine* an[d] a very successful production of the international h[it] *Vagina Monologues*.

1993-94

MONDAY WORKSHOPS: On the Theatre's 'day off[',] 4-hour sessions were conducted by invitees for a grou[p] of actors who believed that training was important t[o] an actor's growth.

Ansh: Makarand Deshpande has written, produced an[d] directed about 30 plays, including *Ek Kadam Aage, Drea[m] Man, Chitra, Airavat, Kuute Ki Maut, Samrangan, Kastur[i]*

...aila, Basant Ka Teesra Yauwan, Baje Dhol, Sir Sir Sarla and Seema Badnam Hai, and has also acted in some of them.

1993-2000

PLATFORM PERFORMANCES: Held in the Theatre courtyard every weekend, these half-hour outdoor performances for exploring space and new theatrical expression began as Festival occurrences and grew into round-the-year activity.

1994-95

Shashi Kapoor produced an audio cassette (through HMV) of some of the major songs of the Prithvi Theatres.

1995

The first Prithvi Festival to be organised by Sanjna Kapoor, Divya Bhatia and Atul Kumar as Festival Directors in Mumbai and Delhi.
A memorial stamp was released by the President of India on the 50th anniversary of Prithvi Theatres.
The Company Theatre: Set up by Atul Kumar and Sheeba Chaddha, this group has presented works by Ionesco, Stoppard, Molière, Shakespeare, Chekhov, Marivaux, Frayn, and their own theatre creations like *The Blue Mug* and *Yalta Suite for Solo Cello*. They have promoted new theatre directors in laboratory theatre projects. The Theatre Company also introduced the 'Theatre at Home' concept in Mumbai.
PRITHVI GALLERY: After a gap of more than a decade, the Gallery which Sakina and Tyeb Mehta ran for a year in the '80s, has been revived bringing alive the Theatre foyer with art by well-known and unknown artists, 'exhibition' being the chief aim rather than 'sale', with 6-7 exhibitons a year and Prithvi's traditional 'brunch-under-the-bamboo' openings with live music.

1996

PRITHVI THEATRE AT HORNIMAN CIRCLE GARDEN: On the first weekend of every month (barring monsoon months) Prithvi Theatre presents open-air theatre in this enchanting public garden; all shows are free, and attended by a diverse audience.

1997

THEATRE POSITIVE—A SERIES OF PLAY READINGS: This event was born out of a mini-play reading festival titled '... and then there is English Theatre', where 6 Indian-English plays were read over 3 mornings. Theatre Positive was subsequently born. On the first Monday of every month, a new Indian script is read and critiqued. To date over 65 scripts have been read in Hindi, English, Marathi, Gujarati, Malayalam and Punjabi. Theatre Positive was conceived and managed by Ramu Ramanathan.

Saiyan Bhaye Kotwal: Vasant Sabnis' tamasha-style musical *Vichha Majhi Puri Kara*, was done in Hindi by Waman Kandre. A.K. Hangal, Anjan Shrivastav and Javed Khan featured in this musical about a sly minister who tries to take the king for a ride, but is stymied by a clever police constable.

Sambhog Se Sanyas Tak: Satyadev Dubey's frenzied farce set in the distant past, brings up issues of gender politics in a hilarious manner. Princes, ascetics, gods, and commoners, all get caught up in a crazy battle of the sexes, as curses come true, people are reborn, fall in and out of love and chase one another up and down the stage. It was a bedroom farce without a bedroom, as Dubey put it. Starting with Naseeruddin Shah and Ratna Pathak Shah, several actors have participated in the play's umpteen revivals. The play was even done in English by Dubey as *Magic Pill*.

Sangeet Debuchya Muli: The Company Theatre produced Paresh Mokashi's unusual musical about two girls who, after much debate, come to the conclusion that the root of all problems lies in the division of humankind into two sexes. They come to believe that if all men turned into women, these problems would be solved.

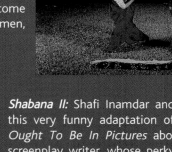

Shabana II: Shafi Inamdar and Daisy Irani did this very funny adaptation of Neil Simon's *I Ought To Be In Pictures* about a Hollywood screenplay writer, whose perky daughter turns up at his doorstep after 16 years and wants to be in the movies. Her arrival turns his life upside down.

Sakubai: Nadira Zaheer Babbar wrote and directed this funny, poignant and wicked satire on contemporary society as seen through the eyes of the humble housemaid Sakubai, played with brio by Sarita Joshi, the prima donna of Mumbai's Gujarati stage.

Sir Sir Sarla: Makarand Deshapande's play is about the strange relationship between a professor, his disciple and the woman who flits in and out of their lives. The professor (Rajendra Gupta) and the student (Anurag Kashyap) are working on a thesis on 'love' and Sarla's (Sonali Kulkarni) visit reopens long festering wounds.

Sganarelle & The Flying Doctor: Atul Kumar, Sheeba Chaddha and their Company Theatre took great pains over the costumes, sets and befittingly exaggerated performances to recreate Molière's farces to perfection.

Tughlaq: Dinesh Thakur did a very lavish Hindi production of Girish Karnad's play about the 14th-century ruler Mohammad Bin Tughlaq, who foolishly shifted the capital of India from Delhi to Daulatabad, made copper coins equal in value to silver dinars and killed his brother, but also cared about the welfare of his people. Thakur played the lead role himself and also designed the sets of this expensive production.

Vagina Monologues: Mahabanoo Mody Kotwal and her son Kaizad brought Eve Ensler's international hit *Vagina Monologues* to India. With a fine cast of Dolly Thakore, Jayati Bhatia, Avantika Akerkar, Sonali Sachdev and herself, she got audiences to accept the 'V' word and empathize with the play's message.

Wah Re Peergulam: Akhil Mishra directed and acted in this Hindi adaptation of Carlo Goldoni's farce *Servant of Two Masters* in which a broken man takes up two jobs with separated lovers on the run, who have landed up at the same inn. Confusion and comedy abound in this crazily paced play.

Woyzek: Pankaj Kapoor and Anita Kanwar acted in this play directed by Ranjit Kapoor, adapted from Georg Buchner's play about a soldier who is ill-treated by an army captain, forced to become a human guinea pig for a doctor and cuckolded by his wife, before he starts off on his own path to redemption.

Yahudi Ki Ladki: This Agha Hashr Kashmiri play in Parsi Theatre style was one of the first plays performed by Nadira Zaheer Babbar's Ekjute in Mumbai. She revived it in 2002, with daughter Juhi playing a lead role, the objective being to give modern audiences a glimpse of the conventions of Parsi Theatre that has had an abiding influence on our popular cinema.

The Keli Festival: The Keli Festival aims to bring the very finest of Kerala's classical performing arts to 'lay' Mumbai audiences in digestible dozes! It is the brainchild of Mr. Ramachandran and run by Keli.

1998

PT NOTES: Since 1998, the monthly newsletter carries theatre news, reviews, discussions, interviews, and the Prithvi Theatre monthly schedule. Subscription is free.

1999

THE INTERNATIONAL PUPPETRY FESTIVAL: This is a bi-annual event. Prithvi Theatre is one of the partners along with Alliance Française, British Council and Max Mueller Bhavan, promoting puppetry as an art form beyond the traditional notion of it being for children.

Ideas Unlimited: Manoj Shah is one of the few directors today doing offbeat plays in Gujarati—*Master Phoolmani, Akha Akhabolo.*

Working Title: Jaimini Pathak's group has a very fruitful association with playwright director Ramu Ramanathan, with plays like *Combat, Curfew, Mahadevbhai* and *Arabian Nights.*

2002

PLAY READING GROUP: This was begun by a group of enthusiasts led by Ramu Ramanathan to read and discuss various playwrights' works. These readings take place every Monday evening.

DHAMAL: The brainchild of Satyadev Dubey, this was a experiment on the first Monday of every month opening up the stage to encourage a wide range of forms of theatrical expression.

Cultural Heritage Series: Under the aegis of this new title, Prithvi Theatre hopes to present to Mumbai a wide variety of performances demonstrating the diversity and significance of performing traditions, both 'old' and 'new'. It is the Theatre's firm belief that in strengthening one's roots and gaining a good sense of where one 'belongs', a confident contemporary voice can emerge.

2003

THEATRE MATTERS—FILM SERIES screens films related to theatre—documentaries and films based on play scripts. The idea is to explore, appreciate and enjoy theatre through the medium of film.

2004

FOCUS FESTIVAL: A new initiative begins with these focus festivals where one aspect of theatre would be in focus through performances, exhibitions, seminars, film shows in order to forge a deeper understanding and appreciation.

Index

Suggested Reading

Anand, Mulk Raj. *The Indian Theatre*. London: Dennis Dobson, 1950.

Aspects of Theatre in India Today. New Delhi: Ministry of Scientific Research and Cultural Affairs, 1960.

Awasthi, Suresh. *Drama, The Gift of Gods: Culture, Performance and Communication in India*. Tokyo: Tokyo University Institute for the Study of Languages and Cultures of Asia and Africa, 1983.

Benegal, Som. *A Panorama of Theatre in India*. New Delhi: Indian Council for Cultural Relations, 1967.

Chattopadhyaya, Kamaladevi. *Towards a National Theatre*. Bombay: All India Women's Conference, 1945.

Contemporary Playwriting and Play Production. Delhi: Bharatiya Natya Sangh, 1961.

Das Gupta, Hemendranath. *The Indian Stage*. 4 vols. Calcutta: Metropolitan and M.K. Das Gupta, 1934-44, (Reprinted as *The Indian Theatre*. Delhi: Gyan, 1988).

Dass, Veena Noble, *Modern Indian Drama in English Translation*. Hyderabad: V. N. Dass, 1988.

Dhingra, Baldoon. *A National Theatre for India*. Bombay: Padma, 1944.

Dayal, Professor Jai. *I Go South With Prithviraj Kapoor*. Bombay: Prithvi Theatres Publication, 1950.

Gargi, Balwant. *Theatre in India*. New York; Theatre Arts, 1962.

———. *Folk Theatre of India*. Seattle: University of Washington, 1966.

Ghurye, G.S. *Indian Costume*. Bombay: Popular Prakashan, 1966.

Gokhale, Shanta. *Playwright at the Centre: Marathi Drama from 1843 to Present*. Calcutta: Seagull, 2000.

Gowda, H.H. Anniah (ed.). *Indian Drama*. Mysore: University of Mysore, 1974.

Gupta, Chandra Bhan. *The Indian Theatre*. New Delhi: Munshiram Manoharlal, 1991.

Indian Drama. New Delhi: Publications Division, Ministry of Information and Broadcasting, 1956. (Second edition, 1981).

Iyengar, K.R. Srinivasa (ed.). *Drama in Modern India and the Writer's Responsibility in a Rapidly Changing World*. Bombay: P.E.N. All-India Centre, 1961.

Jacob, Paul (ed.). *Contemporary Indian Theatre: Interviews with Playwrights and Directors*. New Delhi: Sangeet Natak Akademi, 1989.

Jain, Nemichandra. *Indian Theatre: Tradition, Continuity and Change*. New Delhi: Vikas, 1992.

———. *Asides: Themes in Contemporary Indian Theatre*. New Delhi: National School Of Drama, 2003.

Kendal, Felicity. *White Cargo: A Memoir*. Michael Joseph, 1998.

Kendal, Geoffrey. *The Shakespearewallah*. Sidgwick and Jackson, 1986.

Lal, Ananda (ed.). *The Oxford Companion to Indian Theatre*. Oxford University Press, 2004.

Lal, Ananda and Sukanta Chaudhuri (eds.). *Shakespeare on the Calcutta Stage: A Checklist*. Calcutta: Papyrus, 2001.

Lal, Ananda and Chidananda Dasgupta (eds.). *Rasa: The Indian Performing Arts in the Last Twenty-Five Years: Theatre and Cinema*. Calcutta: Anamika Kala Sangam, 1995.

Mehta, C.C. (ed.). *Bibliography of Stageable Plays in Indian Languages*. Baroda: M.S. University, 1963.

Nadkarni, Dnyaneshwar. *The Indian Theatre*. New Delhi: Shri Ram Centre for the Performing Arts, 1999.

Narasimhaiah, C.D. and C.N. Srinath (eds.). *Drama as Form of Art and Theatre*. Mysore: Dhvanyaloka, 1993.

Pandey, Sudhakar and Freya Taraporewala (eds.). *Studies in Contemporary Indian Drama*. New Delhi: Prestige, 1990.

Proceedings of the 1956 Drama Seminar. New Delhi: Sangeet Natak Akademi, n.d.

Rangacharya, Adya. *Indian Theatre*. New Delhi: National Book Trust, 1984.

Sajjan, Sunder and Satya. *Shri Prithvirajji Kapoor Abhinandan Granth*, Bombay: Triveni Rangamanch Prakashan, 1960.

Sarat Babu, M. *Indian Drama Today: A Study in the Theme of Cultural Deformity*. New Delhi: Prestige, 1997.

Segal, Zohra and Joan L. Erdman. *Stages: The Art and Adventures of Zohra Segal*, Kali for Women, 1997.

Shah, Anupama and Uma Joshi. *Puppetry and Folk Dramas for Non-formal Education*. New Delhi: Sterling, 1992.

Shastri, Acharya Jankivallabh. *Prithviraj Kapoor: Abhinandan Granth*. Allahabad: Paramarsh Mandal, 1963.

Sinha, Biswajit. *Encyclopaedia of Indian Theatre*. 3 vols. Delhi: Raj, 2000 and continuing.

Subramanyam, Lakshmi (ed.) *Muffled Voices: Women in Modern Indian Theatre*. New Delhi: Shakti, 2002.

Theatre in India. Paris: International Theatre Institute, n.d.

Theatre India 1977. Trichur: Kerala Sangeet Natak Akademi, 1977.

Varadpande, M.L. *Invitation to Indian Theatre*. New Delhi: Arnold Heinemann, 1987.

———. *History of Indian Theatre: Loka Ranga; Panorama of Indian Folk Theatre*. New Delhi: Abhinav, 1992.

Varadpande, M.L. and Sushil Subhedar (eds.). *The Critique of Indian Theatre*, Delhi: Unique, 1981.

Vatsyayan, Kapila. *Traditional Indian Theatre: Multiple Streams*. New Delhi; National Book Trust, 1980.

Yajnik, R.K. *The Indian Theatre; Its Origin and Its Later Development under European Influence, with Special Reference to Western India*. London: Allen and Unwin, 1933.

Yarrow, Ralph. *Indian Theatre. Theatre of Origin. Theatre of Freedom*. Richmond: Curzon, 2001.

ISBN: 81-7436-348-3

Text: © Roli Books Pvt. Ltd.
Photographs and visual materials:
© Prithvi Theatre

Layout: Naresh Mondal
Production: Naresh Nigam

© Roli & Janssen BV 2004
Published in India by
Roli Books in arrangement
with Roli & Janssen BV, The Netherlands
M-75 Greater Kailash-II (Market)
New Delhi 110 048, India.
Phone: 91-11-29212271, 29212782
Fax: 91-11-29217185
Email: roli@vsnl.com
Website: rolibooks.com

Printed and bound in India